KU-795-051

Site and Composition

Site and Composition examines design strategies and tactics in site making. It is concerned with the need for a renewed understanding of the site in the twenty-first century and the need for a critical position regarding the continued tendency to view the site as an isolated 'fragment' severed from its wider context.

The book argues for revisiting the traditional instruments or means of both siting and composition in architecture to explore their true potential in achieving connections between site and context. Through the various examples studied here it is suggested that such instrumental means have the potential for achieving greater poetic outcomes. The book focuses on the works of twentieth-century architects of wide-ranging persuasion – Peter Eisenman, Le Corbusier, Frank Lloyd Wright, Alvaro Siza, Herzog & de Meuron and Charles Correa, for example – who have strived in quite different ways to achieve deeper engagement with the physical qualities of place and context.

Departing from a reconsideration of the fragment, *Site and Composition* emphasises the role of the 'positive fragment' in achieving both historical continuity and renewed wholeness. The potential of both planimetric and sectional compositional methods is explored, emphasising the importance of reciprocity between 'inside' and 'outside' – between fragment and the whole, as well as materiality. Written in a clear and accessible manner, this book makes vital reading for both researchers and students of architecture and urbanism.

Enis Aldallal has been practising architecture in the United States since 2011 and is pursuing licensure in the state of Illinois. Before coming to the USA, he practised architecture for six years in renowned architectural firms in the Middle East. He holds a MArch from Illinois Institute of Technology (2011) and an MPhil from the University of Liverpool, UK (2009). His interest in place-specific approaches to architecture supports his research on site-related challenges and how they engage with his architecural designs.

Husam AlWaer is an urbanist with a background in architecture, urban design and sustainability. He is Senior Lecturer in sustainable urban design and evaluation in the School of Social Sciences, University of Dundee, having previously researched and taught at Reading and Liverpool universities. Husam's work has had considerable impact in academia, practice and in the field of community out-reach. With Barbara Illsley he is currently editing *Place-making: Rethinking the Master-planning Process*, with contributions from internationally reputed scholars and experts in the field (ICE Publisher, expected 2016).

Soumyen Bandyopadhyay holds the Sir James Stirling Chair in Architecture at the University of Liverpool. Director of the research centre, ArCHIAM (Architecture and Cultural Heritage of India, Arabia and the Maghreb), he has published widely on aspects of Indian modernity and vernacular architecture of Arabia. His recent publications include *The Territories of Identity* (Routledge 2013, co-edited with Guillermo Garma-Montiel) and *Manah: Omani Oasis, Arabian Legacy* (Liverpool University Press 2011).

Site and Composition
Design strategies in architecture and urbanism

Enis Aldallal, Husam AlWaer and Soumyen Bandyopadhyay

Routledge
Taylor & Francis Group

LONDON AND NEW YORK

First published 2016
by Routledge
2 Park Square, Milton Park, Abingdon, Oxon OX14 4RN

and by Routledge
711 Third Avenue, New York, NY 10017

Routledge is an imprint of the Taylor & Francis Group, an informa business

British Library Cataloguing in Publication Data
A catalogue record for this book is available from the British Library

Library of Congress Cataloging-in-Publication Data
A catalog record for this book has been requested

ISBN: 978-0-415-49825-8 (hbk)
ISBN: 978-0-415-49826-5 (pbk)
ISBN: 978-1-315-73037-0 (ebk)

Typeset in Myriad Pro
by Karen Willcox, www.karenwillcox.com

Printed and bound in India by Replika Press Pvt. Ltd.

Contents

vi   Enis Aldallal | Site and Composition: Design strategies
Husam AlWaer and | in architecture and urbanism
Soumyen Bandyopadhyay |

Illustrations

Preface

The book is concerned with the need for a renewed understanding of the site in the twenty-first century and the establishment of a critical position regarding the continued tendency to view the site as a fragment severed from its wider context. The dominant modernist tendency to regard the world around as a fragmented phenomenon, which replaced the world of pre-modern certainty, has been found inadequate in the postmodern era of globalisation, and amidst a renewed interest in achieving wholeness. Even as we have to treat sites increasingly as assemblages of orthogonal projections – which has no doubt helped designers often operating remotely in today's globalised world of architectural practice – such abstraction need not necessarily prevent us from considering the deeper, often latent and less obvious knowledge about the site. Instrumentality and abstract codification *per se*, we argue, are not the problem, and, as Alberti's survey of Rome demonstrates, are even critical to our understanding of orders of things. It is the counter-creative and anti-anthropological manner in which we have increasingly treated such material that has caused the crisis.

Addressing these tendencies, this book has argued for revisiting the instruments of both siting and composition in architecture to explore their true potential in achieving connections between site and context. Departing from a reconsideration of the fragment, and the processes that form fragments, fragmentation, the book emphasises the role of the 'positive fragment', and the role such *positive* entities could potentially play in achieving both historical continuity and renewed wholeness. It focuses on architects of wide-ranging persuasion of the twentieth century – for example, Peter Eisenman, Le Corbusier, Frank Lloyd Wright, Alvaro Siza, Herzog & de Meuron and Charles Correa – whose works defy categorisation under simple binary oppositions. Through the various examples studied here, we suggest that the instrumental means have the potential for enhanced analogical and scalar relationships capable of achieving poetic outcomes. By considering such architects' works of diverse periods and geographical locations, one intention is

to question the lenses of preconception through which their works are regarded and promptly put into artificial 'political' categories. However, more importantly, it is a plea to treat architecture and the city *not* as a collection of disjointed objects but as overlapping networks of relationships, cutting across temporal and cultural boundaries.

We would like to thank all those who have helped the long journey of this book from an initial idea to fruition. Our sincere thanks to those who read and commented on the initial proposal, including Professor Graeme Hutton; special thanks are due to Professor Nicholas Temple who read and commented extensively on an earlier draft of the book. Thanks are also due to Desiree Campolo and Manwinder Lall for preparing the illustrations for publication; Desiree has worked tirelessly to ensure that all photographs are of uniform quality and has helped prepare a number of drawn illustrations that accompany this book. The North American material was collected through fieldwork visits to the key buildings discussed in this book, helped by numerous individuals: Frank Lloyd Wright's Robie House in Chicago; Zaha Hadid's Contemporary Arts Centre in Cincinnati; and Peter Eisenman's Aronoff Centre for the Arts in Cincinnati and the Wexner Centre for the Visual Arts in Columbus. Some of the Indian material on Le Corbusier and Charles Correa was collected during the course of an Arts and Humanities Research Council (AHRC) supported research on modernity in Indian architecture and Nek Chand's Rock Garden in Chandigarh. OTTO Archive, Richard Brook, Clive Gracey and Dr Ana Souto have kindly permitted the use of their photographs of the following buildings: Douglas House in Harbor Springs, Michigan; CaixaForum in Madrid; a traditional mosque in Manah in Oman; and the Galician Centre for Contemporary Art in Santiago de Compostela. Dr Iain Jackson has permitted the use of photographs of a drawn illustration of Chandigarh city plan and photographs of the Mill Owners' Association Building in Ahmedabad. Fondation Le Corbusier has kindly allowed us to use reproductions of photographs and drawings by Le Corbusier and of his sketchbook pages.

004   Enis Aldallal | Site and Composition: Design strategies
Husam AlWaer and | in architecture and urbanism
Soumyen Bandyopadhyay |

For various reasons this book has been a long time in the making. We would like to acknowledge the continued patience of the editors and designers at Routledge for their support of this project. Earlier ideas on Le Corbusier's design approach in Chandigarh involving fragments were presented at the 2009 'Architecture and Justice' conference held at the University of Lincoln, and a preliminary study of reciprocity in the Mill Owners' Building in Ahmedabad was published earlier in 2007. We would like to thank Professor Tom Jefferies and the Manchester School of Architecture at Manchester Metropolitan University for the support extended towards the publication of this book. Last but not least, we would like to extend our heartfelt gratitude to our families, as without their continued support the book would not have materialised.

1 Introduction:
site and composition

The need to revisit our understanding of the site and its relationship to its surroundings has become necessary – more than ever before – at this point well into the twenty-first century.

Such a necessity has arisen for a number of reasons. The reality is that site considerations have received progressively less attention in the academic and professional practice of architecture over the past decades. The proliferation of iconic buildings – Venturi's *ducks*[1] – has resulted in distinctive, formally unique architecture, claiming special symbolic and aesthetic qualities. Formal iconicity has also been proclaimed and acquired through the unbuilt, such as in Libeskind's proposed extension to the V&A Museum in London and Alsop's Fourth Grace project in Liverpool. Aspiring to be the object of veneration itself, such iconicity is removed from previous understandings of the term as representation or resemblance of a sacred persona or work of art generated following established conventions. This solipsistic isolation and narcissism has often resulted in little attention being given to the qualities of their sites, and the building and site's relationship to the surroundings. Venturi's *decorated shed*, exemplified by the myriad out-of-town shopping complexes and neighbourhood supermarkets, has also remained uneasily situated within a landscape essentially shaped by the need to optimise car-parking arrangements. Contrary to Venturi's belief, these structures housing mundane and everyday activities have hardly carried any enduring symbolism, meaning or social messages, to which the insensitive, banal treatment of site and context have contributed. Sadly, architectural education has not been immune to such developments and pressures.

The welcome rise in environmental concern has also ushered in a kind of myopic, conservative instrumentality into the way both architects and students of architecture are now guided to handle sites. The tendency to assess the appropriateness of a site for building and its relationship with the wider context through a set of overly simplistic and determining criteria – site geometry, orientation, transport and accessibility, solar gain, minimal environmental footprint, community benefits, to name a few – is both limiting and abstract in its scope.[2] On the other hand, rising demand for expediency in building procurement, cost optimisation and the persistent shadow of the conservationists looming large over architects engaged in suburban volume house-building projects have limited the opportunities for engaging with site and context.

The age of frenzied information production and exchange has arguably turned our world into a global village with a flattened geography with no peaks and troughs. More than ever before, architects and architectural practices are working at locations across the globe – and often remotely. The 'foreigner' could potentially bring in a critical dimension – a refreshed dialogue – to energise debate regarding the reshaping of a built environment; however, this is not always the case. Beyond the obvious technical expertise the foreigner adds to the project – the perceived universal applicability of which, in itself, is not bereft of a problematic political dimension – the interventions remain global and are seldom localised due to lack of knowledge of site within specific locales. Perhaps paradoxically, this demand has now been given added impetus by the desperate need for expansion outside the West in the light of the present economic downturn that has changed the architectural profession forever.

Burns and Kahn define the understanding of site under three distinct areas of concern:

> the first … is the area of control, easy to trace in the property lines designating legal metes and bounds. The second, encompassing forces that act upon a plot without being confined to it, can be called the area of influence. Third is the area of effect – the domains impacted following design action.[3]

These concerns have important scalar implications, both in terms of the actual physical extent of the sites but also

008   Enis Aldallal | Site and Composition: Design strategies
Husam AlWaer and | in architecture and urbanism
Soumyen Bandyopadhyay |

in their perceptual qualities – from within and without. The book aims to address this by considering a wide range of scales and definitions of sites. The examples chosen for discussion include, of course, the bounded and defined urban site, of which Le Corbusier's Mill Owners' Association, a building we discuss in some detail, or Herzog & de Meuron's CaixaForum, which we consider in terms of its materiality, are excellent examples. Alvaro Siza's Galician Centre for Contemporary Art, although part of a larger collection of buildings, nevertheless sits on a fairly defined site. Such examples characterise the restricted, or enclosed, urban sites typical of most urban developments in cities. However, recognising the emergent contemporary condition of expansive 'campuses' or 'parks' produced by global corporate developments, many of the case studies included here examine buildings, or complexes of buildings, whose site boundaries or edge conditions are not so clearly defined or, in the extreme case, even non-existent. Peter Eisenman's Wexner Centre for the Visual Arts at the Ohio State University campus and the Aronoff Centre for the Arts at the University of Cincinnati, or the siting of the High Court building within the Capitol Complex at Chandigarh – and even Frank Lloyd Wright's Robie House – are sites that are expansive, with varying degrees of definition, which acknowledge – and are acknowledged by – larger geographical terrains beyond their immediate surroundings. As we will find out, this results, in various ways, in buildings becoming expansive with respect to surrounding land and horizon.

Returning to Burns and Kahn's first concern, the area of control, the most spatially and temporally limiting attribute of a site, is unfortunately regarded as its prime characteristic. The second one is rather more difficult to fathom but remains closely connected to the first. In describing Alberti's attempts at surveying the city of Rome (*Forma Urbis Romœ*) using an instrument he called a Horizon, Leatherbarrow notes how he ignored the terrain between the Capitoline Hill – the position of the instrument – and the city wall, choosing to plot 'key points on the perimeter and

a number of significant places in the expanse between'.[4] The mathematical understanding of the city he thus developed employed an abstract – and thus transparent – matrix, which ignored or temporarily suspended the consideration of the in-between terrain. Although known extremely well through everyday lived experience of the city, for Alberti the substrate could be seen to have withdrawn 'into a kind of darkness, a blind spot, remaining latent and unnoticed'.[5] Leatherbarrow highlights this inversely proportional nature of the relationship between the refined and abstracted nature of the mathematical (instrumental) and the latent existential knowledge of the site. The mathematical method of 'seeing *through* things', more often through orthogonal projections such as plans and sections, does not necessarily need to reject the 'tacit thickness of things' – the knowledge that eludes instant enumeration.[6] This thinking provides the central thrust of the book.

The above unfolds a number of issues central to this book. Alberti's treatment of the city was evidently not homogeneous, for the potent latency of the middle ground also gave prominence to selected structures and buildings – urban fragments consisting of buildings situated on sites – which appeared as positive, projected figures within a recessive backdrop.[7] Yet these fragments were never extraneous to the city, never able to evade the influencing omnipresence of the urban context. The context thus not only surrounds a site but pervades and permeates all aspects of it; the urban fragments perform within an un-homogeneous – viscous – field of relationships that create a tacitly acknowledged wholeness. That the site should indeed be regarded as a *fragment of a wider whole*, connected by intense and reciprocal relationships between the site and its context – between overlapping fragment and the whole – forms part of the central argument of this book. Indeed, wholeness was once better understood – within traditional and pre-modern environments – and fragmentation was essentially a product of modernity. Today, a refreshed understanding of the fragment and the processes that manifests it –

fragmentation – is therefore necessary for the restoration of a renewed wholeness.

This book also highlights the importance of optimising the potential of the existential and the instrumental relationships between a site and its context, which we undertake mainly – but not exclusively – through the work of Peter Eisenman in the United States from the late-1970s and Le Corbusier in India in the 1950s. The choice of architects, apparently with such diametrically opposed tendencies as Le Corbusier and Eisenman, requires some explanation. The categorisation of architects and their works into modern, postmodern, Neo-Rationalists, and so on, to begin with, is extremely problematic. Such divisions are essentially temporal classifications of convenience rather than evocative of distinct intellectual orientations. Eisenman's works of the 1980s and 1990s have carried forward concerns central to modernists in their heyday, as did Le Corbusier's post-Second World War projects anticipate postmodern concerns well before its formal proclamation. The projects cited in this book, we believe, transcend these artificial boundaries and are not necessarily or solely 'modern' or 'postmodern' in their orientation. The works of architects as geographically removed as Neutra and Correa from the 1950s demonstrate sensibilities that ventured way beyond the premises established by normative modernism. The evolved postmodern sensibility is crucial to our position, as it helps us re-evaluate trajectories of historical development in understanding relationships between site and architecture, and question ideas of progress, as well as problematic aspects of order and hierarchy (of both ideas and buildings).

In spite of their obvious differences, the works of both Le Corbusier and Eisenman show remarkable interest in the constructed nature of the site and in methods of reading these. Both have focused on the historical and mytho-poetic contents that sites and their contexts offer and have searched for methods of first de-constructing and later re-constructing them as part of the design process. For

Le Corbusier, the site had to be reduced to the irreducible fragments or the resilient cultural remains – its historical and poetic essence, and an artificial datum established by the deposition of the accumulated detritus. These fragments and the datum provided the armature for his architecture to explore and provide measure for issues of cultural and social significance, helping the architect to adopt a polemical position. If Le Corbusier's approach is about clarification through reduction, Eisenman's approach, resisting reduction, sought decadent immersion in the opulence of the site's historically and culturally layered nature. Through a series of largely unbuilt experimental projects from the late-1970s he identified the crucial importance of composition as the basis for re-establishing multivalent relationships between site and its urban and regional contexts. The artificial, playful assembly of the archaeological/topographical layers through the infusion of narratives is the basis of this reconstructive process. Their works and methods locate them at two extremes of a spectrum; overt instrumentality characterises Eisenman's process, while Le Corbusier's instrumental moves – employing drawings and texts – have largely operated from his sketchbooks.

Especially at Ronchamp but also in Chandigarh, Le Corbusier had moved away significantly from the typological and technological concerns of the 1920s towards a pronouncedly existential take on architecture. His sketchbooks were glyptic recordings of experiences joined up through mathematical notations, which appear to be simultaneously alluding to the abstract 'high-altitude thinking' and the 'mundane horizon and … individual action'.[8] The mundane outline using textual fragments – barely revealing a profile – encoded a depth of experiences, an approach also identifiable in his high-altitude landscape sketches representing archipelago of selected topographic fragments spaced out by expanses of white. For Le Corbusier, such textual and drawn recordings were economic means of representation, analogous to plans and sections. Like the employment of oppositions in his work, fragments spaced

010   Enis Aldallal | Site and Composition: Design strategies
Husam AlWaer and | in architecture and urbanism
Soumyen Bandyopadhyay |

out yet connected by abstraction 'provoked his imagination, his creativity, and his myth making'.[9]

The implied possibility – or at least, the promise – of orthogonal projections to return to the 'thickness of things', in effect highlights the analogical and scalar relationships that exist – and could exist – between the fragment and the whole. The instrumental and the existential, traditionally the domains of rationalists and phenomenologists, respectively, have featured in the projects and proposals of some architects of the late twentieth century. Their drawings 'consist very often of no more than fragments of potential objects, which come to exist only through the process of transformation and projection – or to use the architect's words, "deconstructive constructions".'[10] While the latter term refers to Daniel Libeskind's description of his own work, the method of using transformational drawings – anamorphosis using projective geometry – has also been an important tool for Peter Eisenman, especially between 1978 and 1988, when he produced a cohesive body of work under the title *Cities of Artificial Excavation*.[11] Eisenman employed methods of repeated tracing and overlapping, and varied scalar impositions as tools for unearthing histories, questioning memories and revisiting the notion of composition, the latter long considered the means of relating site to its context. Instrumental methods, aptly employed, could therefore act as vital tools of incision that allow views into deeper and imagined realities, both extending our access to the 'thickness of things' by stretching our ability to 'experience, visualise and articulate – in other words to represent so as to participate in the world'.[12]

This approach, however, is not without its critics; in particular, questions have been raised regarding how the combination of a repetitive process and somewhat wilful manipulation of figure–ground relationships that emerge from the conjunction of layers can usefully sustain a collective memory of the urban legacy of site and its relationship to the larger city or region. Such abstract, geometrical manipulations have been criticised as

obscuring the dialogic potential of architecture through what are essentially static, monologic exercises. As we aim to demonstrate later through the siting and design of the Aronoff Centre (see Chapter 4), Eisenman's work deserves a more sympathetic understanding. His work has demonstrated the infinite inventive capacity of geometry to visually construct relationships, which when employed perceptively, could enrich the formal architectural vocabulary. However, behind the bewildering eloquence of composition also lies several both playful and serious attempts at achieving sensitive dialogic relationships, for example, through the technique of *grafting* – the careful implantation of extraneous catalytic fragments.

A fixed view of what constitutes reality has unfortunately limited our understanding of site as merely an 'area of control', and rendered composition – the act of siting buildings – processual, reducing composition to the unquestioned and predictable methods of relating the fragment to the whole. Eisenman's gradual shift away from the solipsistic compositional formality of his early houses (Houses I–IV, 1967–71, built and unbuilt) – where he searched for an autonomous architectural syntax based on the analysis of seminal works of the modern movement by Le Corbusier and Giuseppe Terragni – however, is instructive regarding the evolutionary potential of instrumental compositional methodologies. In House VI (1976) Eisenman relinquished the 'limited range of formal experiments'[13] in favour of a 'new linguistic and semantic sensibility',[14] a transformation complete by the time of House X (1975–77, unbuilt) that engaged with the considerations of the site and the outside. To emancipate composition both from its classical roots as well as its modernist adherence to transformation of ideal typologies, he introduced de-composition, prompting him to replace the cube, 'the preferred generating volume of his first houses, with the fragmentary "el", a three-sided portion of a hollow cube'.[15] In House 11a (1978, unbuilt) the departure from the obsessive certainties of Euclidian geometry to the ambiguities of the contemporary human condition is apparent, with the 'els' assuming quasi-topological qualities – yet retaining the resonance of the archetype it dismantles – heralding a closer link between the building, its site and wider context.

Eisenman's move from the formal to the semiotic and finally, as he claims, to the poetic – moving from composition through decomposition to excavation – indicates a shift from the syntactic to the fictional. It unveils the possibility that composition could be the poetic and fictional exploration of a site's constitution. As such, composition is design that resists making the distinctions Burns and Kahn make between the encompassing forces in action and the impacted domain of influence. The interplay of diverse fragments of spatialities and temporalities, and the interrupted forces of histories, cultures, social motives and structures, of economies and technologies – to name a few – create the essentially non-homogeneous constructedness of sites. The archaeologist Hodder reminds us of two types of contextual meaning; one refers to the 'environmental, technological and behavioural context of action' and the other is to do with the idea of context being 'with-text', thus introducing 'an analogy between the contextual meanings of material culture traits and the meanings of words in a written language'.[16] Crucially, Hodder emphasises the importance of the notion of 'text' over 'language',[17] articulating the text's predilection for content over symbol and as an embodiment of content, to which the language provides supportive infrastructure.

Nothing stands on its own; dichotomies – autonomy/ dependency, harmony/cacophony and fragmentation/ integration – shape both living organisms and man-made systems. Throughout the ages cultures have encapsulated such dialectics through divergent modes of representation – literature, painting, sculpture, architecture and urbanism. It could be argued that the portrayal of our contemporary aspirations as the confrontation between technological revolution and a nostalgia for the past has prevented cultures from recollecting their dispersed and fragmented

bodies of representation. In turn, this confrontation has inevitably exacerbated the representational dilemma, precipitating further and renewed cultural fragmentation. If perceptual wholeness is a quality that is preferable to the human psyche, as one that aids creativity and innovation, then its characteristics require exploration in relation to fragmentation. To restore that wholeness, the discussion will argue that buildings, and especially sites – as fragments of a whole – have the potential to complete a reordering through design by virtue of their latent collective qualities. Fragment is not a shredded, broken-off piece of an object, but a positive entity in a constant state of becoming, which – through manipulation by designing, and the employment of formal language – establishes connections with both other spaces and human actions. Such completion therefore requires reading the site both as a fragment and as part of a wider set of fragments, especially important to the understanding of urban infill, as well as to the methodology of this book.

This book argues for the need to revisit the opportunities offered by the idea of composition – both as constitution and as reordering by combining – to reinvestigate the relationship between site and its wider context for contemporary architecture to return to a new wholeness. The remaining part of this chapter is devoted to understanding the nature of the fragment and the processes of its generation – fragmentation – as well as the ideas surrounding wholeness. The fragment is both 'received' and 'created'; its reverberating, dynamic nature defies severance from its origin or past. The perceptual processes that combine fragments to produce the whole are also discussed. Chapter 2 explores the potential of the fragment by arguing that at the High Court in Chandigarh Le Corbusier employs the primordial fragment to explore the notions of social justice and, thus, truth. This stands in contrast to Charles Correa's employment of temporal or historical fragments to redress balance between cultures at the British Council Headquarters in Delhi. Chapters 3 and 4 analyse how Peter Eisenman, in two of his key built projects belonging to

012   Enis Aldallal | Site and Composition: Design strategies
Husam AlWaer and | in architecture and urbanism
Soumyen Bandyopadhyay

the 'Artificial Excavation' phase, employs planimetric and sectional devices to construct real and fictive relationships between the site and its surroundings. Chapters 5 and 6, using examples from diverse parts of the world, explore how reciprocity between the inside and the outside, as well as materiality, could achieve the wholeness contemporary architecture so desperately desires.

Fragment and fragmentation

In discussing the ambiguous meaning of an object or artwork, André Breton described it as a 'crisis of the object' resulting from its essentially fragmented nature, where 'the object ceases to be fixed permanently to the near side of thought and re-creates itself on the further side as far as the eye can reach'.[18] Analogous to nuclear fission that releases sub-atomic particles into unpredictable, reverberating motion, fragments are volatile; 'and fragmentation is movement'.[19] The crisis of the object described by Breton due to its ambiguous fragmentary nature is also its source of strength; its meaning derived from the constituent fragments. Seen in this way, the fragments are the most enduring and normative conditions, while the totality – the whole – which perhaps there was none, is ephemeral.[20] Discontinuity characterises both the spatiality and the temporality of wholeness, in which the fragment extends between the past and the present and between the near and far grounds of representation: it has a history and a presence.

Since Alberti's assertion that a house is a small city and a city is a large house,[21] the idea has become the maxim for all those who adopted the relational idea of universality and locality. This relationship has emerged as the criterion for evaluating fragmentation or integration in various cultural disciplines, including architecture and urbanism. Over time this has inspired some critics to invent the phrase 'part-to-whole' relationship which, in turn, prompted many designers to claim absolute wholeness in their work and through their representations of the world. However, the

pursuit of absolute wholeness has led to their unavoidably stumbling on fragments.

The desire to study fragments and fragmentation is a product of modernity and traditional societies rarely felt the need to identify a cultural object or text as a disjointed, autonomous fragment. This becomes clear when we consider the role of ruins and relics; while no longer fulfilling their original purpose as permanent places of habitation, ruins on the edge of a village provided places of refuge from the all-devouring darkness of the approaching night, from the natural elements and from the undesirable elements of human society. Not subjected to entropy-defying preservative forces of modern fragmentation, they became temporary sanctuaries of the societal other. The naturally occurring wholeness in vernacular societies was given cohesion through entropy – through death and disorder – from which the modern fragments appear to have found emancipation.

The emergence and acknowledgement of fragments seems to accept a state of severance amidst cultural continuity. Wheeler, in his inspiring study of the place of rituals and relics in Islam, has explored how Muslim scholarship has linked 'selected objects, actions and locations to the origins and development of Islamic civilisation'.[22] One of the examples he cites is the recovery of the treasures (relics) of the Ka'bah.[23] Wheeler argues that the contents of the treasure signify a transition between two fundamentally important states of human existence and society. The recovered treasures and their association with pre-Islamic prophets and kings tie the utopian state of existence in the Garden of Eden to the later condition of Islamic civilisation culminating in the Prophet and the institution of Islam, suggesting the 'received' nature of the relics. This attempt at creating a meta-narrative incorporates Islam and the Prophet into an extended topography of histories, conceptions and prophets going back to Adam and his expulsion from the Garden of Eden.

Fragments are also continually 'created' alongside being received, illustrating the contrasting modalities of their existence.[24] The small cupola atop the prayer halls of central Oman – the *bumah* (Figure 1.1) – derived both its name and its form from the third millennium BC beehive tombs that surround many oasis towns. In Arabic it is also the owl – the cupola perhaps deriving the name from the immobile form of this solitary nocturnal bird silhouetted against the sky. In Arabia the owl has been largely regarded as inauspicious and connected with death, calamity, the spirit or the ghost. The Ibadi Muslims seem to have preferred this diminutive form in their mosques to the towering minaret for the purposes of *adhan* (call to daily prayers). Given the beehive tombs' pre-Islamic origin (the days of ignorance, *jahiliyah*), and its profanity due to the original sepulchral role and association, its incorporation into the sacred mosque in the guise of the diminutive *bumah* suggests a gradual acceptance (reception) and transformation (creation) of a relic from a world forbidden from discussion.[25]

Understanding the phenomenon of fragmentation and its relationship to the idea of wholeness entails tracing their emergence in our modern cultural life, heavily reliant on the oculocentric representation of objects. As Vesely points out, 'the emergence of the fragment as a significant phenomenon can be traced back to the origins of perspective',[26] although its clear manifestation could be detected in the subsequent emergence of the Cubist works of Picasso and Braque produced between 1907 and 1912.[27] Its appearance as a noticeable phenomenon in painting suggested new and unforeseen re-groupings of representations and the world of emergent fragments that were no longer related to a coherent whole, independent from their parts and settings.[28] What usually helps to identify incidents of fragmentation or integration are references to the contexts of their source and destination. Taking for granted that the juxtaposition of fragments as a method of innovation would result in coherence is problematic as 'mere juxtaposition does not inevitably produce aesthetic potentials. The aesthetic response occurs

when attention fragments are combined within the brain to form a "pattern" which has coherence and elegance.'[29] A fragment, in some way, possesses a history linking it to its origin or the place which granted that fragment its structure and identity. Fragments are endowed with characteristics and values resident in the whole,[30] allowing reading those fragments as representatives of their wider context to perform loyalty to the whole. That is why the treatment of fragmentation on a purely formal basis is highly limiting as it neither acknowledges its history nor its present. Consequently, it is not possible to comprehend the fragment in isolation, but only in relation to its settings – whether of dependency or of independence. In other words, fragments always have situational structure defining their position towards themselves and the world. The transplantation of a fragment may potentially lead to a semantic transformation of its new context,[31] which could well have positive or negative impact. Understanding what impact fragmentation is likely to have can be achieved through two essential actions; first, through the method of representation, and second, through references to contexts.

The emergence of fragmentation within modernity made us aware of its exciting transformative and representational potential. Tschumi viewed the phenomenon as a tool for epistemological transformation when he claimed that, 'in its disruption and disjunction, its characteristic fragmentation and dissociation, today's cultural circumstances suggest the need to discard established categories of meaning and contextual histories'.[32] Yet, fragmentation has also led to fragmentary ways of reconstructing and representing our beliefs, resulting in deep cleavages between nature and man and between man and man.[33] Fragmentation has divided our built environment and our thinking about it.[34] The condition is the product of a mentality 'which seizes on isolated elements that can be combined at will, has its origin in the late eighteenth century, when the elements were treated for the first time as real fragments able to generate their own context'.[35] Fragments could be recovered and re-aggregated through a series of

014   Enis Aldallal | Site and Composition: Design strategies
      Husam AlWaer and | in architecture and urbanism
    Soumyen Bandyopadhyay |

Figure 1.1 Diminutive cupola, the *bumah* on top of Omani mosques used for the call to prayer.

surgical procedures according to the designer's intentions. Fragmentation, however, cannot be employed as a tool either to deconstruct the cohesive structure of extant systems or to retrieve their original wholeness. Others, however, have attempted to seek regularity, harmony and continuity – intellectual, physical, social and individual – as a counterforce to the inevitability of fragmentation. For them, for wholeness and harmony to overcome fragmentation, the configuration should depend upon the extent to which unifying elements overweighed disintegrity.[36] What, therefore, is the nature of the new wholeness?

Wholeness

What distinguishes wholeness is the existence of fragmentation. As a reaction to the phenomenon which appeared, as Vesely reminds us, 'as an unwanted guest, a by-product of an underlying tendency in the evolution of modernity',[37] wholeness has reasserted its necessity as a demanding, organising counter-power to the contemporary condition of fragmented representation. Hence, its significance lies in the desire for ordering as a fundamental quality of the human psyche,[38] and only through relationships can wholeness be achieved. To identify the aspects of perceptual wholeness, certain qualities that characterise this phenomenon – unity and diversity, relationship and uniqueness, and context and interiority – require consideration.

Unity includes anything that holds a whole together, that makes it one thing; it contains and sustains systems. *Diversity*, on the other hand, provides options, resources and simulation, resulting in evolution and vitality. *Relationship* connects things and people, and ideas and images, linking together or intertwining them. The power or weakness of the whole lies in the relationship of its parts. *Uniqueness* implies that everything, everyone and every moment has its own identity and characteristics. *Context* is what surrounds us like conditions, forces, structures, and circumstances. Context can even influence events and concepts for

better or for worse. *Interiority* is the content and what is embedded inside us, in systems or larger structures.[39] These oppositional pairs – unity/diversity, relationship/ uniqueness and context/interiority – help evaluate the perceptual wholeness. The unity of the parts emerges from the consideration of whether they develop a single idea or the interrelationship of several ideas.[40] This stance has been addressed in *Gestalt* psychology, which 'considers a perceptual whole the result of, and yet more than, the sum of its parts … it is dependent on the position, number, and inherent characteristics of the parts'.[41] Others have claimed that perceiving wholeness requires taking certain steps, which are 'identifying the parts, specifying the properties of these parts, specifying the relations between them, and specifying the relations between the whole and the parts'.[42] This four-step mechanism has also underpinned certain notions of regularity and beauty, as Smith highlights:

> Beauty consists in a rational integration of the proportion of all the parts of a building, in such a way that every part has its fixed size and shape, and nothing could be added or taken away without destroying the harmony of the whole.[43]

As a first step, in order to perceive 'formal harmony' as beauty, Smith had argued that four basic aspects need consideration: coherence, proportion, internal integration and cosmic integration. Since the classical era the notion of formal coherence has been used to understand the logical shifts between the beginning and the end of an entity that consists of two parts or more.[44] Coherence is in turn influenced by the 'systems of "proportion", which have been more or less axiomatic tend to lay down relationships in which one entity exceeds the other by an amount sufficient to cause acceptable tension but not dominant'.[45] The internal integration results from the unity of parts that give the whole a chance to interact positively with what is outside. Thus the power of a system lies not only in the internal integration of its parts but also through their rapport with the wider context to achieve the cosmic

016   Enis Aldallal | Site and Composition: Design strategies
Husam AlWaer and | in architecture and urbanism
Soumyen Bandyopadhyay

integration. Recognising these aspects opens the door for understanding architecture from an urbanistic standpoint, as Venturi reminds us, by focusing comprehensively on the true extent of its exteriority and interiority.[46] Venturi points out that, while perceptual wholeness is difficult to achieve, attempting to understand the perceptual whole could bring into discussion an entire range of complexity. This complexity lies either in the multiplicity and/or diversity of the parts or in the inconsistency of the weaker parts in relation to the stronger ones.

In disciplines where the visual attributes of a phenomenon make up the main standard of communication, the focus is always on the manner in which they can be represented and perceived. In fact, the understanding of any relationship is significantly influenced by the oculocentric nature of our perception, which stores what we see as images and then converts those into subconscious knowledge. The human mind, in this process, projects most of the data into images

and is 'programmed to seek meaning and significance in all sensory information sent to it'.[47] Relationships of solid/void, vertical/horizontal and enclosure/disclosure are aspects of interrelations that the human mind tries to perceive constantly. The main focus of *Gestalt* psychology is to interpret those pairs in the image of meaningful patterns.[48] According to it, the human mind constantly attempts to find an ultimate command as well as regularity, thus preferring and tending to a status of absolute uniformity. Uniformity consequently seeks an organisational relationship between the entities without dismantling the identity of any. It is important to mention that perceiving the uniformity is not restricted to identical objects and patterns that have the same size, shape, colour and so forth; instead, in terms of scale and function, for example, the variety of functions and elements at a smaller scale is important for perceiving large-scale coherence.[49] Thus the mind perceives organisational relationships in patterns regardless of the 'scale' of the fragments. What best describes such circumstance is the fractal composition, where all fragments have the same properties but differ in scale (Figure 1.2).

The fragment–whole relationship in architecture should eventually result in a meaningful language of expression that relates part to part and parts to the whole through certain criteria.[50] The most common graphical method of representing the fragment within its wider context has been the figure–ground paradigm, exemplified by the simple representation of a Greek vase in *Gestalt* psychology. The drawing in this example illustrates two basic themes; the first, providing a 'ground', is the profile of two human heads facing each other, framing a void, while the latter, offering the shape of a Greek vase, appears as the 'figure' (Figure 1.3). Here, the mind is caught in a dilemma prompted by the illusion presented in this drawing: which one to perceive; the heads or the vase? A third illusion also arises, which is through the attempt to perceive all the fragments collectively at the same time, i.e. reading the heads and the vase as one entity. This phenomenon relies on the triggering of the subconscious knowledge prompted by

Figure 1.2 Natural fractal.

Figure 1.3 Gestalt interpretation of Greek vase.

the figurative indications. Thus, whether it is an artwork or an architectural product, it is the representation that determines our perception. Both present modes of representation which are simultaneously aesthetic and material; however, architecture distinguishes itself by being inhabitable and experiential.

The meaning of an architectural object has a great deal to do with juxtaposition. An object gains in significance when it is located among similar ones in its original context; it gains in symbolic meaning when the juxtaposition takes place away from that context. According to Vesely,

> what is common to all is the reference to the original context to which they represent. The fragment of a building, the torso of a sculpture, an object taken out of its context, and an artificial ruin often initiate 'symbolic meaning' and reference more powerfully than does the piece intact in its original setting.[51]

Therefore perceiving the fragment within the understanding or image of a whole 'depends on possibilities of representation in which a part can be a believable equivalent of the whole or at least a promise of the whole'.[52] Figure 1.4 shows one possibility of a systematic juxtaposition of the Greek vase for the collective set of fragments to read as a balustrade. The above illustration is admittedly overly simplistic, as the opportunities for such a repetitive, systematic occurrence within our built environment are rare. Many architects are also quick to guard against such instrumental productions, which – rightly or wrongly – they fear are limiting in the production of structures and systems supporting human habitation, and that spatial productions, as a result, could be in danger of losing their credibility through extreme regularity.[53]

Fragmentation in architecture

Fragmentation, introduced into modern art through Cubism, soon found similar compositional resonances within techniques of collage production and slightly later in Surrealism. During the early twentieth century, modern movement architecture was trying to be the total architecture and even a totalitarian discipline[54] that intended to replace the Beaux Art style. Yet Douglas Cooper thought that Cubist methods – precisely fragmentation – influenced modern architecture after the First World War.[55] Some two decades later, one of the earliest treatments relating Cubism to architecture appeared in Gideon's book, *Space, Time, and Architecture* (1941). The employment of the fragment and fragmentation in architecture appears to have been manifested through three phases: first, through the revolutionary impulse introduced from Cubism in the 1910s and 1920s; second, through its appearance as a way of humanising modern architecture during the post-war years; and finally, in the period running up to the present that could be termed as the end of humanism and the end of the age of modernity.[56] From the paintings of Cubism to the architecture until the demise of the modern movement,

018   Enis Aldallal | Site and Composition: Design strategies
Husam AlWaer and | in architecture and urbanism
Soumyen Bandyopadhyay |

Figure 1.4 Juxtaposing and repeating the Greek vase to read as a balustrade.

the fragment has appeared 'as an object, as a structure, or as a complete and coherent system'.[57]

From Cubism to Deconstruction the interpretation of fragmentation in architecture has produced ever more complex representations mainly through its appearance, aiming to question the very structure of objects by manipulating the material world through architecture. What distinguishes Deconstruction from other trends is its attempts to find ways of externalising and materialising the chaotic dislocations of Cubism through persistent breakage of the structure of objects, realising imaginal, inscriptive worlds that are impossible to materialise *per se*. It became mainly an exercise in making representation – descriptive drawings and projective geometry – material.[58] Although unable to question the idea of structure, as Tschumi had once supposed, Deconstruction emerged as a practical and positive force.[59]

Architecture can only exist through the world in which it is located.[60] Given its heterogeneous, encompassing organic nature, architecture enters into a constant state of becoming through its fragmentary structures. As Cohen suggested: 'Either consciously or unconsciously, architecture comes to embody the most stable and persistent values of a culture and through this institution becomes symbolised

by their buildings, their values become associated with architectural forms'.[61] The circumstance of becoming makes possible the 'composition, the ordering of objects as a reflection of the order of the world, the perfection of objects, the vision of a future made of progress and continuity … conceptually inapplicable today'.[62] On the urban scale, where systems are much bigger and parts vary in identity, property and relationship, fragmentation is more obvious and palpable.

The belief that both art and architecture could grant shape and meaning to an independent, self-contained framework or fragment is in itself flawed and is evidence of the modern crisis of fragmentation.[63] To be self-contained is to have the entire circumstances and events located within the site and to make those substantial parts of the architectural programme and experience. The emphasis, instead, should be to perceive the site and architecture as a fragment of a potential larger object or whole that endeavours for, physically and culturally, the completion of a higher system of synthesis and virtue. Aldo Rossi's trials to complete the wider structure of a city through its artefacts – monuments, typologies and so forth – contaminated by a monumental interpretation of city structure – had entrapped him in a vicious circle of juxtaposition of images devoid of sense of scale and belonging.[64] Rossi attempted to legitimise it as 'individuality': 'the figure is clear but everyone reads it in a different way. Or rather, the clearer it is the more open it is to a complex evolution.'[65] For him, this individuality had two attributes; first, each artefact had its own history exclusively rooted in its place; and second, its own form was necessarily inherited in its function. Paradoxically and more ambiguously, the radical concern that Rossi had expressed with regard to bringing an object into a new context led him to neutralise his standpoint by adopting Francesco Milizia's position: 'The comfort of any building consists of three principal items: its site, its form, and the organization of its parts.'[66]

Bringing the architectural object into a new circumstance entails inflecting its structure. Considering the notion of reading architecture as a fragment of a certain setting has found unique reverberations in the Prairie style of Frank Lloyd Wright. Venturi commented that,

> in accommodating his rural buildings to their particular sites, he [Wright] recognized inflection at the scale of the whole building. For example, Falling Water is incomplete without its context – it is a fragment of its natural setting which forms the greater whole. Away from its setting it would have no meaning.[67]

Unlike the Prairie style, the modern movement's reading of intervention has idealised site circumstance in a way that presented architecture as fully detached from its unique place and references, leading to its suppression.[68] Idealising site's circumstance presented by the modern movement is not very different from that in our contemporary days. Elizabeth Meyer articulated that 'a range of other concerns, such as abstraction and invention, the autonomy of the art object, mechanistic and technological metaphors, and standardization and mass production, served to marginalize site practices as nostalgic or instrumental'.[69]

020   Enis Aldallal | Site and Composition: Design strategies
Husam AlWaer and | in architecture and urbanism
Soumyen Bandyopadhyay |

Notes

1 Venturi, R., *Complexity and Contradiction in Architecture*, New York: Museum of Modern Art, 1977 (reprint). Also see discussion on the 'iconic' in, Sklair, L., 'Iconic Architecture and Capitalist Globalisation', in Herrle, P. & Wegerhoff, E. (eds), *Architecture and Identity*, Berlin: LIT Verlag, 2008, pp. 210–219.

2 See, for example, Sassi, P., *Strategies for Sustainable Architecture*, London: Taylor and Francis, 2012.

3 Burns, C. & Kahn, A., 'Introduction', in Burns, C. & Kahn, A. (eds), *Site Matters: Design Concepts, Histories and Strategies*, New York and Abingdon: Routledge, 2005, p. xii.

4 Leatherbarrow, D., *Uncommon Ground: Architecture, Technology and Topography*, Cambridge, MA: MIT Press, 2002, p. 5.

5 Ibid., p. 11.

6 Ibid., p. 12.

7 Nicholas Temple's observation provides useful background to this emerging relationship between monuments and the city's abstract order, which ultimately led to the emergence of abstraction in modernity:

> Radical as it was, Alberti's survey was undertaken in the light of a still deeply embedded medieval tradition of the civic (*civitas*), that saw the city as a constellation of symbolic relationships rooted in a mytho-historic worldview. Whilst … [rightly] Alberti's approach seemed largely indifferent to questions of symbolic value of individual buildings or monuments, it is clear that implicit in the project was an intention to redefine in cartographic terms the topography of the city, and its arrangement of venerated buildings/monuments, in much the same way that the perspectival 'scaffold' of a Renaissance painting served to re-situate a sacred event and the inter-relationships between its participating bodies. It is this analogy between actual and pictorial space, during the Renaissance, that serves … as an interesting prelude to the ultimate abstraction of actual and representational space in modernity, of which the treatment of site is largely symptomatic.
>
> (N. Temple, 2013, personal communication)

8 Leatherbarrow, op. cit., p. 16.

9 Ibid.

10 Vesely, D., *Architecture in the Age of Divided Representation: The Question of Creativity in the Shadow of Production*, Cambridge, MA: MIT Press, 2004, p. 319.

11 Bédard, J.-F., 'Introduction', in Bédard, J.-F. (ed.), *Cities of Artificial Excavation: The Work of Peter Eisenman, 1978–1988*, Montreal and New York: Canadian Centre for Architecture & Rizzoli International, 1994, p. 9.

12 Vesely, op. cit., p. 4.

13 Eisenman, P., 'Interview with David Cohn', *El Croquis* 41, 1989, p. 9.

14 Bédard, op. cit., p. 11.

15 Ibid.

16 Hodder, I., *Reading the Past: Current Approaches to Interpretation in Archaeology*, Cambridge: Cambridge University Press, 1986, p. 153.

17 Ibid., pp. 153–154.

18 Breton, A., quoted in Vesely, op. cit., pp. 318, 320.

19 Tronzo, W., 'Introduction', in Tronzo, W. (ed.), *The Fragment: An Incomplete History*, Los Angeles, CA: Getty Research Institute, 2009, pp. 1, 4.

20 Ibid., p. 4.

21 Cited in Tavernor, R., *On Alberti and the Art of Building*, New Haven, CT: Yale University Press, 1998, p. 190.

22 Wheeler, B., *Mecca and Eden: Ritual, Relics and Territory in Islam*, Chicago, IL: Chicago University Press, 2006, p. 11.

23 Bandyopadhyay, S., *Manah, an Omani Oasis, an Arabian Legacy: Architecture and Social History of an Omani Settlement*, Liverpool: Liverpool University Press, 2011, pp. 208–212.

24 Tronzo, op. cit., p. 1.

25 Bandyopadhyay, op. cit., pp. 232–239.

26 Vesely, op. cit., p. 320.

27 Evans, R., *The Projective Cast: Architecture and its Three Geometries*, Cambridge, MA: MIT Press, 1995, p. 57.

28 Tschumi, B., *Architecture and Disjunction*, Cambridge, MA: MIT Press, 1996, p. 180.

29 Smith, P., *The Dynamics of Urbanism*, London: Hutchinson, 1974, p. 74.

30 Vesely, op. cit., p. 325.

31 Tschumi, op. cit., p. 183.

32 Ibid., p. 208.

33 Bohm, D., *Wholeness and the Implicate Order*, London and New York: Routledge, 2002, p. 3.

34 Ellin, N., *Integral Urbanism*, New York and London: Routledge, 2006.

35 Vesely, op. cit., p. 324.

36 Smith, P., *Architecture and the Principle of Harmony*, London: RIBA, 1987, p. 27.

37 Vesely, op. cit., p. 322.

38 Smith, *Dynamics of Urbanism*, p. 76.

39 www.co-intelligence.org/I-wholeness.html, accessed 21 December 2012.

40 Holl, S., 'Questions of Perception: Phenomenology of Architecture', in Holl, S., Pallasmaa, J. & Gómez, A., *Questions of Perception: Phenomenology of Architecture*, Tokyo: A+U Publishing; San Francisco: William Stout Publishers, 2007, p. 119.

41 Venturi, op. cit., p. 88.

42 Meirav, A., *Wholes, Sums, and Unities*, London: Kluwer Academic, 2003, p. 10.

43 Smith, *Dynamics of Urbanism*, op. cit., p. 74.

44 Ibid., p. 75.

45 Ibid., p. 76.

46 Venturi, op. cit., p. 86.

47 Roth, L., *Understanding Architecture: Its Elements, History, and Meaning*, Boulder, CO: Westwiew Press, 2007, p. 67.

48 Ibid.

49 Salingaros, N., 'Complexity of Urban Coherence', *Journal of Urban Design* 5(3), 2000, p. 291.

50 Clark, R. & Pause, M., *Precedents in Architecture: Analytic Diagrams, Formative Ideas*, Hoboken, NJ: Wiley Academy, 2005, p. 239.

51 Vesely, op. cit., p. 322.

52 Ibid., p. 324.

53 Schulz, C.-N. (Nasso, C. & Parini, S., eds; Shugaar, A. trans.), *Architecture: Presence, Language and Place*, Milan: Skira, 2000, p. 225.

54 Evans, op. cit., p. 57.

55 Ibid.

56 Ibid., p. 55.

57 Vesely, op. cit., p. 322.

58 Evans, op. cit., p. 94.

59 Ibid., p. 84.

60 Tschumi, op. cit., p. 176.

61 Cohen, S., 'Physical Context/Cultural Context: Including it All', in Hays, K.M. (ed.), *Oppositions Reader: Selected Readings from a Journal for Ideas and Criticism in Architecture 1973–1984*, New York: Princeton Architectural Press, 1998, p. 66.

62 Tschumi, op. cit., p. 176.

63 Vesely, op. cit., p. 330.

64 Moneo, R., *Theoretical Anxiety and Design Strategies in the Work of Eight Contemporary Architects*, Cambridge, MA: MIT Press, 2004, p. 104.

65 Rossi, A., *The Architecture of the City*, Cambridge, MA: MIT Press, 1984, p. 19.

66 Francesco Milizia quoted in Rossi, op. cit., p. 40.

67 Venturi, op. cit., p. 96.

68 Redfield, W., 'The Suppressed Site: Revealing the Influence of Site on Two Purist Works', in Burns, C. & Kahn, A. (eds), *Site Matters: Design Concepts, Histories and Strategies*, New York and Abingdon: Routledge, 2005, p. 190.

69 Meyer, E., 'Site Citations', in Burns, C. & Kahn, A. (eds), *Site Matters: Design Concepts, Histories and Strategies*, New York and Abingdon: Routledge, 2005, p. 117.

2 Resilient fragments

Introduction

While designing the foyer of the Pavillon Suisse (1932), Le Corbusier found success in composing with fragments, an aspect he recounts in the *Œuvre Complète, 1929–34*. This, as Peter Carl points out, became an important device in the architectural formulations of his late phase and appears to have played a key role in such buildings as the chapels at La Tourette and Ronchamp, at Chandigarh and the Philips Pavilion.[1] At Shodhan House, Ahmedabad, he employs an especially prominent bulbous projection at the north-eastern corner of the entrance facade to house the toilets designated for the domestic hands. A similarly prominent – but larger – curvilinear volume is repeated on the first floor for the guest bath, this time visible through a horizontal slit in the facade. Both are secondary programmatic components (servants' toilets and guest bath) that have been given prominence through a formal device incongruous with the otherwise orthogonal spatial arrangement. In associating distinctive formal devices – or fragments – with 'peripheral' functions and thus rendering those a prominence, Le Corbusier appears to be interrogating prevailing societal prejudices. At the Mill Owners' Association (Figure 2.1), by apportioning locational and formal prominence to yet another fragment – the toilets at two successive levels, cupped between a pair of

Figure 2.1 Le Corbusier. The Mill Owners' Association Building, Ahmedabad: entrance facade.

026   Enis Aldallal | Site and Composition: Design strategies
Husam AlWaer and | in architecture and urbanism
Soumyen Bandyopadhyay |

curvilinear enclosure walls and held together by a column passing through them – the institutional spatial hierarchy and therefore its *raison d'être* was being questioned, pointing instead to the iconic prominence of the machine at the heart of wealth creation in Ahmedabad (see Chapter 5). Yet again, a larger fragment – the womb-like meeting room – is located at close proximity, to which the toilets form an embryonic adhesion; the fragments present a genealogy through scalar differentiation, yet an indication also of mutual support.[2]

It would appear that Le Corbusier's late architecture in India is engaged with addressing the issues of social stratification and hierarchy, and the role of institutions within a broad spectrum of concerns surrounding social justice and their evocation in architecture. In *Poème de l'Angle Droit* he employs the Open Hand as a metaphor for an open society that is free to interact, 'Open to receive/Open also that others/might come and take', 'it is open because/all is present available/knowable'.[3] Fragments – vertical, erect – play an important role. For him, the right angle (*l'angle droit*) stands for rectitude, 'Categorical/right angle of character/the heart's spirit',[4] produced from the clarity of the heart and mind.[5] At the Mill Owners' the fragments are situated within a three-dimensional orthogonal grid – a giant scaffold that rises from a plateau elevated above ground, supported by the 'deposition' of subordinated servant programmes forming ground and foundation. The plateau – a clarificatory datum that heightens the presence of the fragments placed above – engages directly with the horizon across the river Sabarmati; the latter here drawn into an intense relationship through the grid of sun breakers, which introduces geometry as a device for measuring both horizon and depth of field. The Shodhan House employs a similar device to hold the fragments; only its plateau is divided into a series of interconnected levels. Fragments, datum, geometrical measure, the horizon and the sun are the ingredients of this architecture in Ahmedabad; together they appear to articulate Le Corbusier's

understanding of truth and societal justice set within a unique cultural encounter.

This chapter extends the discussion in Chapter 1 on sites as fragments, and our longing for wholeness, which, one could argue, exists only as a result of the preponderance of fragments in modernity and the myriad processes of fragmentation. Through the analysis of Le Corbusier's work in Chandigarh in India, a different understanding of the fragment–whole relationship is presented. Contrary to the idea of breaking apart, at Chandigarh fragmentation was understood as a clarification through reduction to its resilient cultural/primordial essence. An artificial datum or a grid was introduced as a device to further clarify and foreground the 'archipelago' of fragments, forcibly burying the once-encumbering detritus (which included the many villages that once stood on the city site). The fragments at Chandigarh and Ahmedabad suggest the presence of meta-narratives: they are both historical and yet ahistorical – primordial, *positive* entities capable of achieving renewed wholeness. This denuded primordial armature, in conjunction with the datum that formed a framework for measuring against, made possible the exploration of issues of social justice that appears to have been at the heart of Le Corbusier's High Court building in Chandigarh. Like the tapestries hanging behind the judge's seat that helped complete a common man's transformation into this elevated position, the new architecture stretched over the fragments like a garb. The High Court illustrates various architectonic measures to connect distant topographic features – mountains, intervening landscape and the horizon – as part of Le Corbusier's attempts to integrate the new city with its natural surroundings. Despite these attempts, the relationship between the Capitol Complex and its surroundings remained problematic, giving rise to Nek Chand's Rock Garden, which serves as a mytho-poetic counterpart to Le Corbusier's parliamentary complex.

In this chapter we explore this notion of justice and the role of the architectural fragment in its contextualisation,

Figure 2.2 Le Corbusier. The High Court Building, Chandigarh: courtroom facade.

mediation and representation in independent India by addressing the case of Chandigarh as the capital of the then newly formed Indian state of Punjab, a city design generally attributed to Le Corbusier. This we do through analysing the design of the courtrooms at the High Court building in Chandigarh, but also in the conception of the central terrace of the Capitol Complex (Figures 2.2, 2.3). The Constitution of India, the supreme law that came into being following India's independence in 1947, had recognised justice, liberty, equality and fraternity as the fundamental principles on which the sovereign, democratic republic of India was founded. The concepts of secularism and socialism, embedded within the Indian Constitution from its inception, were later articulated through the 42nd amendment introduced in 1976.

028   Enis Aldallal | Site and Composition: Design strategies
Husam AlWaer and | in architecture and urbanism
Soumyen Bandyopadhyay |

Figure 2.3 Le Corbusier. The Capitol Complex, Chandigarh: view of the Assembly Building from the High Court.

The chapter contends that Le Corbusier's Indian work was largely concerned with the understanding of truth. His attempts at achieving a renewed wholeness through the architecture played a crucial role in this. This also paralleled his contemporaneous exploration of the 'right angle' in his significant text, *Poème de l'Angle Droit*, as symbolic of action emanating from a discerning, true knowledge, in turn a product of rectitude of mind in communion with nature. Truth for him was universal, which in architecture he naturally associated with primordial architectonic fragments – salvaged from the huge, meandering confusion of history – denuded of their unnecessary encumbrances. The introduction of a datum – the *tabula rasa* – was thus necessary as the clarificatory device in dialogue with the

horizon and nature. Justice was seen as articulated in two ways; in both, an understanding of measure was pivotal. First, as the measure of difference these fragments establish from their historical antecedents, usually undergoing a violent process of severance. And second, through their harmonic integration with nature – measurable through the play of temporal rhythms, but also usually through the incorporation of light and temporal symbolism. At the High Court in Chandigarh a further device has been employed in connection with the discharging of justice – the tapestry that simultaneously provides a woven topographic backdrop for the judge's seat and is a robe that elevates the individual to a role of judgement, vesting the person with the authority of meting out justice. Le Corbusier's work is ahistorical. The universal and secularised principles of justice represented in the planning and architecture of Chandigarh, especially that of the Capitol Complex, has remained at odds with history and the deeply entrenched age-old local practices and beliefs. However, as we contend, in introducing the tapestries into the courtrooms, combined with the impossibility of denuding the fragments entirely of their history, the confusion of history is reintroduced; the implications of this in the design of the Capitol are far-reaching.

We suggest that this conflict was initiated well before the planners and architects were chosen, as administrators of the newly formed Punjab state decided to acquire several villages and associated agricultural land for the purpose. Approaches and means of rehousing these groups, and also those displaced from West Pakistan, were ambiguous at best. This a-priori creation of a *tabula rasa*, we argue, fitted well with Le Corbusier's approach towards integrating modernity with traditional cultures. This integration, for Le Corbusier, takes place through the dissolution of the everyday traditional city, leaving behind a real invincible historical core to be incorporated into the Cartesian grid of the modern city. Le Corbusier regarded the grid and the Capitol Complex as integral with nature, and similarly invincible. However, Le Corbusier's impressionistic recordings of the local, we argue, go beyond the mere incorporation of inert relics; these were seen as essential 'garments' which elevated the universal to the status of the exalted.

The persistent shadow of injustice

It is important to emphasise at the outset the collaborative nature of the master plan's evolution, as Evenson, Sarin, Kalia and, more recently, Perera[6] have demonstrated. Quite clearly, much was at stake in the construction of the new city and it involved not only the high officials of the newly formed Indian state of Punjab, which had lost its traditional capital, Lahore, to West Pakistan, but attracted the direct involvement of the first Prime Minister of India, Jawaharlal Nehru. The views on Indian modernity expressed by Nehru are often oversimplified in a frequently used de-contextualised quotation from his inaugural speech at Chandigarh, suggesting that he desired a city 'symbolic of the freedom of India, unfettered by the traditions of the past … an expression of the nation's faith in the future'.[7] In fact, as Perera suggests, arising out of a deep and strong understanding of Indian history, his position was much more complex yet dynamic,[8] as illustrated by the following,

> there can be no real cultural or spiritual growth based on imitation … true culture derives its inspiration from every corner of the world, but it is home-grown and has to be based on the wide mass of the people. Art and literature remains lifeless if they are continually thinking of foreign models.[9]

Nehru advocated an indigenous development of the plan or at least one involving foreign architects with a deep understanding of the Indian context, which led to the appointment of Albert Mayer as its original planner. However, his views often clashed with those of the Punjabi officials who were more inclined towards a European modernity. Following the death of Matthew Nowicki, Mayer's principal associate, the officials were able to appoint Le Corbusier.

Conflict between local and regional justice, and a nationalistic agenda that foregrounded the need to secure a replacement of Lahore, was prominent in the violent appropriation of the site even before the planners were appointed. The act certainly sought to underscore the symbolic importance of upholding 'the valiant spirit of the Punjabis', as Nehru suggested in his inaugural speech, by associating the city with the location of the temple dedicated to Goddess Chandi, embodying *shakti* (power). At least 27 villages and hamlets were destroyed to make way for the new city, resulting in the eviction of 6,000 people; an even wider area of 58 villages of 21,000 inhabitants and 22,000 acres of cultivated land was also acquired by the government under the Land Acquisition Act of 1894 (Figure 2.4).[10] The legacy of rural inhabitation had persisted when work began on the Capitol Complex, as Yosizaka recounted on his first visit to Chandigarh towards the end of the autumn of 1952,

> earthen farm-houses stood in the vicinity.… In the middle of all this scene was a giant banyan tree, casting a cool shadow. There was a stone-rimmed well just beside it.[11]

However, the suggested nationalistic imperatives were hardly upheld through land acquisition and planning gestures and, instead, a new datum – an abstract, platonic and universal *tabula rasa* – was created for the Capitol Complex as Le Corbusier took over, denuded of any local (i.e. historical) or nationalistic association. The temple of Goddess Chandi, after which the city was named, was not incorporated; meanwhile, the debris from the removed villages accumulated nearby. The wider agenda of housing the displaced population from West Pakistan was treated at best with ambiguity, as Nehru's cautionary note to Mayer would suggest.[12]

The fragments from the destruction of the villages found a more permanent – but initially secret – abode in the Rock Garden at the base of the Capitol hill (Figures 2.5, 2.6).

030   Enis Aldallal | Site and Composition: Design strategies
Husam AlWaer and | in architecture and urbanism
Soumyen Bandyopadhyay |

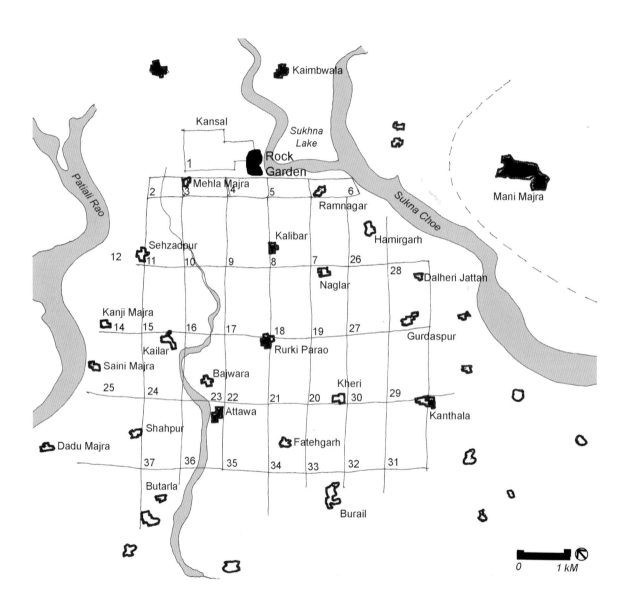

Figure 2.4 Chandigarh master plan: sector organisation showing the many villages and hamlets destroyed through the establishment of the city.

Figure 2.5 Nek Chand Saini. The Rock Garden, Chandigarh: view of a passage.

This 'other' Chandigarh, in effect inverting all the rules on which the city was founded, emerged surreptitiously in the shadows of the High Court as the Capitol Complex neared completion.[13] The Garden's prolonged illegal status until the mid-1970s indicates its problematic positioning within the Chandigarh schema. Its persistent otherness as the complex and vital repository of fragmentary reminders of local histories and representations of life appears to have been vital in the construction of the Capitol's identity by establishing a continual 'measure' of difference.[14] The distancing of the temple of Goddess Chandi from the city named as her 'abode' or 'seat' (*garh*) could equally be seen as providing a measure of

dissociation between 'form' and 'matter'. To these we shall return shortly.

The rise of the fragment and 'measure'

This attempt at establishing a *tabula rasa* by consigning the local to the status of mostly non-essential relics shoved under an impervious and abstracted cartographic datum, and the notion of a 'measure' emerging from the difference between the ideal and the real – between 'truth' and 'history' – appear to have their origins in Le Corbusier's early perception of the Orient and the experience of Istanbul during a fire on the night of 23 July 1911. Embarking on his travels to the East in 1911, Le Corbusier speculated:

> I want Stamboul to sit upon her Golden Horn all white, as raw as chalk, and I want light to screech on the surface of domes which swell the heap of milky cubes, and minarets should thrust upward, and the sky must be blue.[15]

Istanbul, however, presented a different reality: 'Why is Stamboul so grey? Stamboul should be all white and the

Figure 2.6 The Rock Garden: wall detail showing salvaged fragment from earlier inhabitation.

032 Enis Aldallal | Site and Composition: Design strategies
Husam AlWaer and | in architecture and urbanism
Soumyen Bandyopadhyay |

mosques radiant and the light should stream with colours and not be wan and faded', he disappointedly remarked to Karl-Ernst Osthaus on arrival.[16] Yet he never appears to have lost belief that the eternal and true Orient lay hidden and emerged briefly above the foggy shroud that hung over Istanbul in the early hours of the day.[17] Views of the skyline of Istanbul painted during this visit employ the horizontal, reinforcing this idea of the datum as a device for extracting the essential (Figure 2.7). There, foreground and depth coalesced into an agglomeration of fragments of varying densities, providing only a shadowy indication of what lay buried.

The fire in the Old Town of Istanbul Le Corbusier witnessed on the night of 23 July 1911 that destroyed neighbourhoods and dwellings further highlighted this perception (Figure 2.8). His initial expression was a chromatic impressionistic one which, as I shall show later, is also a device he employs in studying the local in India:

> At the horizon, the sky is getting dark and changes from emerald green to a deep ultramarine diluted with green like a glaucous sea. Against it, the minarets and domes of Bayazit are outlined in a splendid unity, incomparably majestic, carved out of solid gold.[18]

Yet this 'dissolution' of the city in the conflagration, as Kries suggests, seems to have also intensified his perception regarding the real core of this Oriental city, its permanent foundation:

> every mortal's dwelling is of wood, every dwelling of Allah is of stone [the city] sheds its skin in this way every four years [and] only the great mosques remain invincible.[19]

Perhaps in Istanbul Le Corbusier first realised the importance of the horizontal as an abstract device for foregrounding the modern city as a representation of the 'truthful' nature of modernity, consigning the confusion of the traditional city into the depths of its topography. This reduction of the past to what he would consider an invincible – irreducible, truthful – core that consisted of salvaged essential fragments, he later applied to Algiers, tearing down almost 60 per cent of the traditional city (the *casbah*), and also to Rio and Buenos Aires.[20]

It is important to note the pivotal role of the reduced fragments in the conception of Le Corbusier's modern Oriental city, and Chandigarh had none as he arrived on the scene. The purificatory reductions appear to be associated with and achieved through violent means, actions and

Figure 2.7 Le Corbusier. 1911. Skyline of Istanbul; watercolour on blue paper, 9 × 29.5 cm.

Figure 2.8 Le Corbusier. 1911. Photograph taken of the fire of Istanbul on the night of 23 July 1911.

events, i.e. resulting from conflagration, by highlighting the prevalence of disease and epidemics in traditional cities and through planning interventions that Edmund Brua described as 'architectonic bombardment'.[21] They indicate distancing through extraction and therefore indicate a reliance on measure.

The drawings he prepared of Algerian women, based on postcards he had collected, show deliberately denuded bodies as if to retrieve the truthful fragments. Truth is 'simple and naked/yet knowable',[22] their retained closeness to the ground – to earth – is recognised.[23] Intensely grouped bodies are captured foregrounding a nomadic tent from which they have emerged (Figure 2.9). Such emergence appears to have parallels with the rising of the invincible fragments of Istanbul above its foggy shroud, ornamented by the brief passage of light every day. The tent, often used interchangeably by Le Corbusier with the cave to represent

034 Enis Aldallal | Site and Composition: Design strategies
Husam AlWaer and | in architecture and urbanism
Soumyen Bandyopadhyay |

Figure 2.9 Le Corbusier, after 1931. Drawing based on collected postcard of nomadic tent in the Algerian desert; graphite and coloured pencil on cardboard, 24.5 × 32 cm.

the sacred shrine,[24] is also here the secular repository of 'culture', to the depths of which the bodies will once again be reconsigned.[25] Here again, brief illumination of the body fragments should be noted, denoting these as the battleground between the universal forces of nature and darkness of the chthonic space. Their distancing from the chthonic context is measurable – both through their illuminated foregrounding, as well as the degree of violent cultural severance the bodies have undergone. The ambiguity posed by the treatment of the cave as both a sacred and a cultural repository is significant, and poses

questions regarding whether shearing off the cultural histories of primordial spatial fragments is ever feasible. The drawing therefore also presents a genealogy of primordial fragments (body, cave/tent), differentiated by scale, as we have noted at Le Corbusier's Ahmedabad buildings.

Analogous to ancient foundation rituals, Le Corbusier's fragments of the eternal city are thus predicated on the deposition of cultural historical detritus. In Chandigarh, 'measure' appears to have become similarly embedded through an incident Yoshizaka reports, when Le Corbusier

Figure 2.10 The Assembly Building: detail of 'Modulor Man' impression on a pylon.

lost his hand-made Modulor roll, kept normally in a film can; this was later reported as 'Le Corbusier's Modulor sown into Chandigarh soil'.[26] History for Le Corbusier, as Carl contends, citing *Poème de l'Angle Droit*, is a 'dialectic between confusion and truth (between deviation and assertion of straightness – *droiture*)',[27] between meander and trajectory.[28] 'The truth is present/only in some spot where the current [of the river water] always seeks out its bed!'[29] The fragments provide the 'obstacles' in the meandering and confused fluidity of history to 'trigger' truth, the eternal presence,[30] yet they are also inevitably formed by the actions of the fluid passage. The fragments thus are the battlegrounds between truth and history – the former measurable through the struggle between light and darkness, as we also notice in the Algerian drawing.

An 'archipelago' of fragments

At the Mill Owners', activated by the machine – suggested by the giant iconographic presence of the pinion of a water mill – the meander of the fluid carves the interior.

The gradual dissolution of its interior fabric (cladding, settings) is a result of what would appear to be an uninterrupted fluid flow down the access ramp, rendering the orthogonal volume into a cave-like interior (see Chapter 5).[31] Both in Ahmedabad and Chandigarh such large-scale primordial fragments are employed to cocoon smaller fragments. At the Capitol Complex an 'archipelago of architectural fragments'[32] of such scale and proportion rise above the *tabula rasa* – 'the terrestrial plain of things knowable', 'edged with horizon/Facing the sky'.[33] Standing erect on the plain they are thus in 'solidarity with nature' and 'fit for action',[34] the edifices where the notion of truth is explored and measured. Significantly, however, although they rise from the violent processes of history (destruction of villages, partition), unlike the fragments of Stamboul or Algiers, they are not salvaged or clarified but instituted and therefore artificial – without a history. This apparent triumph of the ahistorical, and the promise of the clarified primordial fragment is, however, shortlived, as even a cursory glance at the Assembly Building and High

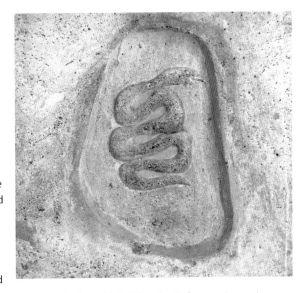

Figure 2.11 The Assembly Building: detail of serpent impression on a pylon.

036   Enis Aldallal | Site and Composition: Design strategies
Husam AlWaer and | in architecture and urbanism
Soumyen Bandyopadhyay |

Figure 2.12 Le Corbusier. The Secretariat Building, Chandigarh: view of front facade.

Court, as well as his Ahmedabad buildings, reveals their debts to Western and Indian classicism. The impressed near-Egyptian representation of the Modulor Man on one of the Assembly pylons, as well as the 'serpentine' representation of history on another, indicate the contaminating existence of pre-history alongside nature and natural history (Figures 2.10, 2.11). These articulate Vidler's assertion that modernists struggled to shed all traces of nostalgic flavour to the fragment in their anxiety to move away from the nineteenth century's 'unhealthy investment' in the past.[35] Fragments, Vidler writes, are characterised by scale, context and narrative; they are part of a world of 'scaled elements', for which the human body

provides the reference; they indicate a context from where they will have been initially 'snatched' and, consequently, they carry forward traces of narratives.[36]

There are three giant fragment types at work at the Capitol Complex: the wall (the Secretariat), the cave (Assembly and Tower of Shadows) and the tent (High Court); together they form a landscape which is 'both coming into being and passing away (reminiscent of a field of ruins)' (Figures 2.12–2.14).[37] Facing each other across the podium and both representing what Carl describes as 'agonic' settings, i.e. 'situations of conflict and decision',[38] the Assembly and the High Court present opposed architectural conditions, indicative perhaps of their differing roles. The former is a 'closed cuboid cave', holding within it two further

Figure 2.13 Le Corbusier. The Tower of Shadows, Chandigarh.

Figure 2.14 The Assembly Building: view of the southwest facade.

chthonic elements (the lower and the upper houses of the Assembly) – opposed in their architectural and symbolic qualities. The enclosed nature of the Assembly hall is given greater prominence with the columns disappearing into the unfathomable darkness of the ceiling painted black. The interior is highly intense, packed with fragments and other interpenetrating architectural elements, which Jencks has termed 'compaction composition even more compacted'.[39] Jencks has suggested the intense interior as Piranesian in nature[40] – alluding in all probability to its parallels with the *Carceri* images – an important observation given the legislative nature of the building. However, these suspended fragments and intense composition could also be read as the iconic symbol of an industrial setting (given to the making of law). The circular-plan lower chamber

(Legislative Assembly) at podium level is crowned by a large, hyperbolic shell that allows sunlight to play with the acoustic clouds along its base. Two of the large fragments – the Assembly and the Tower of Shadows – literally expose the depth of the plateau within their interiors, indicating an intense archaeological interest, reminiscent of his painting capturing the skyline of Istanbul and the accumulated nature of the intervening 'cultural' field. This topographic revelation through recesses in the earth enhances the suspended quality of the lower chamber. The suspended smaller cuboid of the upper chamber (Governor's Council), with its pyramidal roof, is held in place by the orthogonal grid structure. The distinction between the crowning elements – one representing human civilisation of the past (pyramid) and the other of the future (cooling tower) – is

038 Enis Aldallal | Site and Composition: Design strategies
Husam AlWaer and | in architecture and urbanism
Soumyen Bandyopadhyay |

obvious. What is less obvious, perhaps, is a comment on the perpetuation of colonial governance structures and the defunct nature of the upper chamber. As Jencks notes, in an attempt to remove hierarchical organisation, Le Corbusier abolished the speaker's platform, increasing the opportunity for debate. In the true democratic spirit, each 'orator' was provided with a microphone to interrupt legislative proceedings, if necessary.[41]

The High Court, in contrast, is an 'open tent' with the subordinated cave-like fragments exposed to the podium and facing the Assembly, reminding us of the tent foregrounded with bodies in the Algiers drawing, drawing closer the analogy between Corbusian bodies and chthonic receptacles. As opposed to the classically organised facade of the Assembly, the possible influence of Mughal and other Indian precedents on the over-scaled 'parasol' entrance portico (darwaza) has been noted, which comes to an abrupt end at the administrative 'wall'. Here, the 'tent' holds the cave-like volumes of the courtrooms; the openness of the building further enhanced by the direct access given to the courtrooms from the podium. In Chandigarh, Le Corbusier realised that 'the sun was not only a friendly Mediterranean play of light but also the principal adversary in a battle':[42] 'The sun master of our lives/far from indifferent/He is the visitor – an overlord/he enters our house', and, 'brutally/he breaks it twice –/morning and evening'.[43] The battle was thus entered invoking the aid of the brise soleil, the sun-breaker, its shield encrusted with the painted yellow horns of the bull; the horns appear to be also present atop the hyperbolic tower to ward off the sun's rage (Figure 2.15). The numerous photographs of the courtroom interiors attest to the efficacy of the brise soleil, although glare was not completely eliminated, leading some of the judges to switch 'the operation of the courts around, placing themselves against the brilliant light. How could you tell if the accused were lying if you could never see his face because of the glare?'[44] At the High Court the sun breakers, however, established a more intimate relationship with the horizon, reminding us of the Mill Owners' and further

Figure 2.15 The High Court Building: detail of the High Court facade.

enhancing the grounded nature of the cave-like courtrooms. This, combined with the lateral western light, created an important distinction through the play of temporal rhythm from the top-lit and reflected light receptacle of the law-making Legislative Assembly; the enhanced horizontality aligning here with the meting out of justice to the people of Punjab and Haryana. Given the originally intended orientation of the courtroom, the horizontality of the brise-soleil will have given the judge the opportunity to calibrate the extent of deviation from the ultimate truth of nature.

The horizontal has the ability to distinguish the fragile from the invincible, as it provides opportunity for integration with nature. The displacement or extension of the horizon through numerous benches, tables, ledges, parapets and other horizontal furniture devices within the architecture illustrate this reciprocal intention. Le Corbusier conceived of the Capitol Complex as the permanent foundation of Chandigarh, intending the buildings to remain invincible in the face of natural and calamitous change. Conceived thus, the buildings were seen as part of the extended natural landscape, unchanged and unyielding. In his many preparatory sketches for the Capitol, Le Corbusier aspired for its reconciliation with the surrounding Shivalik Hills as a legitimising and redeeming gesture (Figure 2.16). For him, the hills surrounding Chandigarh were material manifestation of absolute order and therefore it was only

logical that his primordial fragments formed part of the narrative of a topographic phenomenon – emerging or perhaps receding. His fascination with aerial views of vast landscape formations that first surfaced with his maiden voyage to South America in 1929 forged a new relationship between the abstracted grid – that diverted the Chandigarh plan away from Mayer's conception – and the surrounding natural features. On the other hand, long-distance perspectives were used to visualise his architecture with a foreground grid, fixing those permanently to the topography through what he termed 'the inexpressible space; impossible to dimension' (Figure 2.17). Here, urban design assumes that the city is in perpetual making, delivered through the continual experience and habitation of an embryonic urbanising intervention.

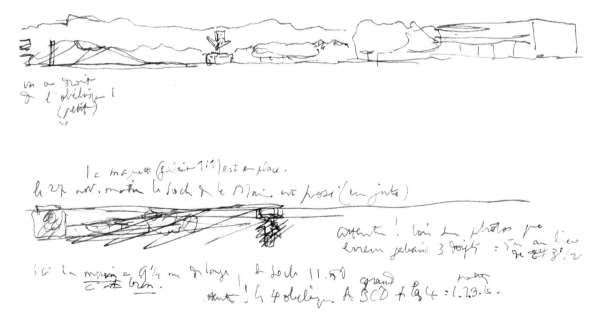

Figure 2.16 Le Corbusier. Sketchbook drawing (213) showing the buildings and installations of the Capitol Complex in the context of the surrounding hills.

040   Enis Aldallal | Site and Composition: Design strategies
Husam AlWaer and | in architecture and urbanism
Soumyen Bandyopadhyay |

Figure 2.17 Le Corbusier. Sketchbook drawing (209) showing foreground grid used as a device to connect the built fabric to the natural topography.

Tapestry as *vêtement*

Removal of the cultural 'fabric' through disrobing (Algiers drawing) or dissolution and redundancy (Mill Owners') is a method Le Corbusier employs to arrive at his irreducible, primordial body/fragment. The opposite – a re-garbing – seems to have been at work in his reconciliatory gesture towards artefacts of everyday culture, giving them renewed iconographic status as reminders of the context from which the primordial fragments were originally extracted. The chromatic encrustation of the *brise soleil*, especially with the bull motif already discussed, forms part of a repertoire of

re-garbing. The giant enamel-painted door at the Assembly is essentially a curtain facing east that highlights the significance of the horizon (complete with its undulating hills) in distinguishing between the subterranean cultural deposition and the eternal rhythm established by the solar passage (Figure 2.18). It is this solar clock that gives rise to the 'sun-breaker'[45] where it is most required – the western facade of the High Court. This re-garbing is extended into the court interiors, where giant tapestries form the backdrop for the judges' seats (Figure 2.19). The chromatic impressionistic recording of the local, simultaneously giving rise to an abstract – almost mathematical – containing analytical structure, was a key feature of Le Corbusier's sketchbooks, for which the following is a good example:

2 Sikh types on bicycle. // colours: turbans – green // – red + some white (or pants? // underneath)? +: the basis of the colour equation, // it's the shirt W which is 'broken' – black – red – white // authorise variation according to the <u>quantities</u> of red // [authorise variation according to] nature [of red] // mix value 40%

There could be equation), black + yellow ochre + white // in [black] green + [white] // [in black] blue + [white][46]

The reduction of the local into a mathematically classified collection of symbolic chromatic and figurative relics – the latter perhaps best represented in the bull horns Le Corbusier studied so exhaustively – we would argue, allowed its later subsumption, subjugation and framing within the universal. In Chandigarh, the abstract grid refined through the use of the Modulor as an expression of the universal and the natural, is all-pervasive. Le Corbusier employed this containing arrangement to structure his canvas for the subjective and selective representation of the local.

However, here we would argue that some of these representational devices are more than relics. David Leatherbarrow, citing Paul Claudel's description of the essential in the Japanese house, suggested that the traditional house in Japan is 'less a box than a vesture (*vêtement*, in French), an apparatus for living and breathing'. He asks:

What if a person or artefact were stripped of its 'vestment'? Without robes a priest or judge would be (again) just like you and me, not only ineffective in ecclesiastical or judicial affairs but also only an individual. Not only is power an attribute of the person who has been vested, but so is a particular kind of anonymity; during the trial no one in the

courtroom knows the judge's name, afterward no one cares. By means of the vestments this person becomes that office.[47]

The chromatic applications at the High Court – derived from his intuitive observation of the local – are, in effect, such vestments employed to elevate the universal – the ordinary – to the role of the specific and the exalted. The double columns of the entrance portico are combined, gunnite sprayed and painted to give it the appearance appropriate for its special role. The tapestries Le Corbusier designed for the individual courtrooms – which provided the backdrop for the judge's chair – were inspired by his observation of the tattered curtain, that fragile piece of ruined fabric he observed and noted in his sketchbook, which provided 'an Indian [brand of] Héraclite comfort'. Thus a quintessentially local element was elevated as a garb for the highest place of the judiciary. Extending beyond the

Figure 2.18 The Assembly Building: detail of ceremonial door.

042   Enis Aldallal | Site and Composition: Design strategies
Husam AlWaer and | in architecture and urbanism
Soumyen Bandyopadhyay |

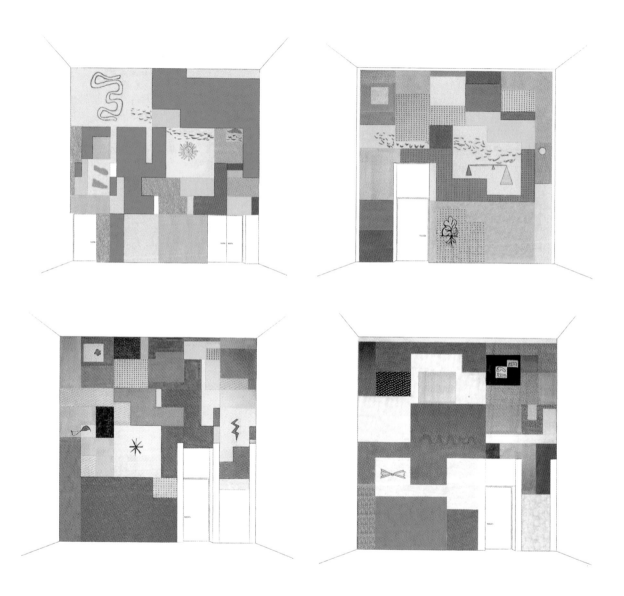

Figure 2.19 The High Court Building: tapestry in the courtrooms.

Figure 2.20 The Rock Garden, Chandigarh: feminine figures draped in broken glass bangles.

objects of potential misfortune into colourful drapes on his anthropomorphic sculptures. The tragedy attached to most of the discarded materials is in this way reversed as Chand transforms the objects while retaining their original use as vestment. The bangles once worn on the arms as symbols of femininity and puberty are now writ large and enrobe the body; they become the girl. They confront the audience – primarily Indian, hailing from the strictures of the male-dominated society. They face the audience in their multitude, which seldom the girls could in their own societies. They ask questions.

relic, the strategic emplacement of the local accentuating the universal indicates an important understanding of social justice within the universality of Chandigarh's planning and architecture.

A similar vestment or garbing is employed by Nek Chand at the Rock Garden to empower his feminine figures (Figure 2.20). A group of the sculptures is clad in thousands of coloured glass and plastic bangles that have been salvaged. The bangles relate to the huge multitude of girls who once lived, and are possibly still living, in Chandigarh. Broken bangles retain misfortune, prompting the owner to discard them forthright. Chand transforms these

044   Enis Aldallal | Site and Composition: Design strategies
Husam AlWaer and | in architecture and urbanism
Soumyen Bandyopadhyay ▌

Notes

1 Carl, P., 'The Tower of Shadows', in Architectural Association, *Le Corbusier and the Architecture of Reinvention*, London: Architectural Association, 2003, p. 102.

2 Some aspects of the Mill Owners' Association building I discuss in Chapter 5 and also in Temple, N. & Bandyopadhyay, S., 'Contemplating the Unfinished: Architectural Drawing and the Fabricated Ruin', in Marco Frascari, M., Hale, J. & Starkey, B. (eds) *From Models to Drawings: Imagination and Representation in Architecture*, London: Routledge, 2007, pp. 109–119.

3 Le Corbusier (Hylton, K. trans.), *'Poème de l'Angle Droit'*, Section F3: Offering (The Open Hand), in Architectural Association, *Le Corbusier and the Architecture of Reinvention*, p. 94.

4 Ibid., Section E3: Characters, p. 90.

5 Ibid. 'She is rightness child of/limpid heart present on earth/close to me'.

6 Evenson, N., *Indian Metropolis: A View Toward the West*, New Haven, CT: Yale University Press, 1989; Sarin, M., *Urban Planning in the Third World: The Chandigarh Experience*, London: Mansell, 1982; Nihal Perera, 'Contesting Visions: Hybridity, Liminality and Authorship of the Chandigarh Plan', *Planning Perspectives* 19(2), 2004, pp. 175–199.

7 See, for example, Southall, A., 'Circle and the Square: Symbolic Form and Process in the City', in Nas, P. (ed.), *Urban Symbolism*, New York & Leiden: Brill, 1993, p. 386; Tan, T. & Kudaisya, G., *The Aftermath of Partition of South Asia*, London: Routledge, 2000, p. 190.

8 Perera, op. cit., pp. 179–184.

9 Nehru, J., *The Discovery of India*, Calcutta: Signet Press, 1946, p. 564.

10 Kalia, R., *Chandigarh: The Making of an Indian City*, New Delhi: Oxford University Press, 1999, p. 12.

11 Yoshizaka, T., 'Chandigarh: A Few Thoughts on How Le Corbusier Tackled His Work', in *Le Corbusier: Chandigarh, The New Capital of Punjab, India 1951–*, Tokyo: A.D.A. Edita, 1974, p. 2.

12 'there is one fact to be borne in mind, and I hope it does not come in the way of your general planning. This is to make provision for the displaced persons from West Punjab.' Jawaharlal Nehru, letter to Mayer, 23 May 1950, in Kalia, R., *Chandigarh*, p. 35, also cited in Perera, op. cit., p. 183.

13 Bandyopadhyay, S. & Jackson, I., *The Collection, the Ruin and the Theatre: Architecture, Sculpture and Landscape in Nek Chand's Rock Garden, Chandigarh*, Liverpool: Liverpool University Press, 2007.

14 It is therefore no coincidence that both represent the work of outstanding creative individuals – Le Corbusier's articulate 'international' approach sharply contrasted by Nek Chand's introspective 'local' outlook.

15 Le Corbusier (Žaknić, I., trans.), *Journey to the East*, Cambridge, MA: MIT Press, 1987, p. 85; also quoted in Kries, M., 'S, M, L, XL: Metamorphoses of the Orient in the Work of Le Corbusier', in von Vegesack, A., von Moos, S., Rüegg, A. & Kries, M. (eds) *Le Corbusier: The Art of Architecture*, Weil am Rhein: Vitra, 2007, p. 170.

16 Kries, op. cit., p. 170, citing Le Corbusier's letter to Karl-Ernst Osthaus, dated 28 July 1911.

17 Ibid., p. 172, citing Le Corbusier's (Charles Édouard Jeanneret) letter to Charles L'Eplattenier, dated 18 July 1911.

18 Le Corbusier, *Journey to the East*, op. cit., pp. 156–157, also quoted in Kries, op. cit., p. 173.

19 Le Corbusier, *Journey to the East*, ibid., p. 98, also quoted in Kries, op. cit., p. 173.

20 Kries, op. cit., pp. 166–167, 174–175.

21 Eduard Brua quoted in Kries, op. cit., p. 168.

22 Le Corbusier, *'Poème de l'Angle Droit'*, Section G3: Instrument, p. 96.

23 Ibid., Section E3: Characters, p. 90.

24 See, for example, Le Corbusier *'Poème de l'Angle Droit'*, Section C2, p. 78:

> For home from home is/in the great cavern of/sleep that other side of/life at night. How/rich alive is night in the/warehouses collections/libraries museums of/sleep! A woman passes./Oh! I was sleeping, forgive me!

25 Carl, op. cit., p. 104, where he also cites lithographs for G2 and G4 of *Poème de l'Angle Droit* by Le Corbusier to support his assertion regarding the interchangeable use of the tent and the cave.

26 Yoshizaka, op. cit., p. 4.

27 Carl, op. cit., p. 108.

28 Le Corbusier, 'Poème de l'Angle Droit', Section A4: Environment, p. 66.

29 Ibid.

30 Ibid.

31 This dissolution is discussed in Temple & Bandyopadhyay, op. cit., p. 114, where the parallels between the entrance facades of the Mill Owners' and the rock-cut cave at Karle are noted (p. 114); see Chapter 5.

32 Carl, op. cit., p. 106.

33 Le Corbusier, 'Poème de l'Angle Droit', Section A4: Environment, p. 64.

34 Ibid.

35 Vidler, A., Warped Space: Art, Architecture, and Anxiety in Modern Culture, Cambridge, MA: MIT Press, 2001, p. 151. Vidler describes the nineteenth-century Romantics' obsession with the ruin – fractured and affected by the ravages of time, but also indicating 'a possible world of harmony in the future'. These ideals were subsequently tempered by, on the one hand, Ruskin's indication at the improbability of both a return to the past and any authentic restoration, and Violet-le-Duc's view that restoration could finally complete the fragment in its 'previously unrealised perfection'.

36 Ibid., p. 153.

37 Carl, op. cit., p. 106.

38 Ibid., pp. 102, 105.

39 Jencks, C., Le Corbusier and the Tragic View of Architecture, Harmondsworth: Penguin, 1987, p. 154.

40 Ibid., p. 155.

41 Ibid.

42 Carl, op. cit., p. 114.

43 Le Corbusier, 'Poème de l'Angle Droit', Section A1: Environment, p. 60.

44 Jencks, op. cit., pp. 156–157.

45 Le Corbusier, 'Poème de l'Angle Droit', Section B4: Mind, p. 74.

46 Le Corbusier, Le Corbusier Sketchbooks, London: Thames & Hudson, sketchbook N56, entry 296, p. 6, January 1959 New Delhi; 31 March 1959 Chandigarh.

47 Leatherbarrow, D., Uncommon Ground, Cambridge, MA: MIT Press, 2002, p. 149.

3 Site readings

Introduction: site as an urban fragment

Many of the dialectical oppositions we associate with a city are a result of the interaction between its environment and its inhabitants; for Rossi, 'the contrast between particular and universal, between individual and collective, emerges from the city and from its construction, its architecture'.[1] Such interactions are often translational, in the sense that their impact is not confined to an event, a specific location or scale, but its effects could be perceived at other locations and at differing scales of operation. In Gerrit Rietveld's view that in a chair are the ideas for a house, and in a house the ideas for a city, lies the indication of integrity between the apparently disjointed urban fragments – from the smallest piece of domestic furniture to the biggest city artefact. Such interrelationships, however, are often ignored by artificially erected disciplinary boundaries between architecture, urbanism, landscape architecture and art. This divide, as Patrick Schumacher once stated, has obstructed innovation in architecture and urban planning: 'They exist as two separately institutionalized practices arresting each other in mutual deadlock.'[2] Rem Koolhaas has expressed a similar view, lamenting the self-centred attitude within architecture: 'Urbanism is something that creates potential, and architecture is something that exploits potential.… Urbanism is generous, and architecture is egotistical.'[3] Leatherbarrow, on the other hand, has highlighted the ways in which both architecture and landscape architecture contribute to the wider, unified cultural framework of topography.[4] Through the lens of the site, links between such disciplines could be reinforced to achieve the wholeness amidst the tendency towards fragmentation and the autonomy of the fragment (see Chapter 1). Site is the palpable organism ready to be experienced, for 'it only exists, in its visual and spatial relation to people, through the introduction of the building which establishes a permanent relation between people and site'.[5] Architecture could well form the fulcrum of a relationship that extends between the city and its most minute artefacts, on the one hand, and between urbanism and art, on the other.

To understand the fragment–whole relationship, two representational tools will be examined; first, the figure–ground relationship, and second, sectional analysis. Both tools help in our understanding of what the overlap of space and action between architectural sites actually means. Overlap also entails considering the term boundary as a central idea to the urban infill. Moving from art to architecture to urbanism, the discussion will identify boundary as the 'communicative space' which accommodates the overlap both instrumentally, as well as in its socio-cultural dimension.

Site-by-site and figure–ground relationship

On the importance of reinforcing the interrelations between sites, Smith argues that the strength of a town or a city structure lies in embodying the principle of creative, reciprocal coexistence of its artefacts. He argues 'a town is "sequential" in its perceptual impact. Its strength lies in the principle of relationship, and as such it has almost a moral potential in countering the present movement towards fragmentation. The wholeness of city can interject this principle into man as an individual and society as a whole.'[6] The understanding of the sequential impact between city artefacts entails awareness of the notion of infill, which is underscored by the need for including the perceptual characteristics of the local physical setting into the understanding of the site.[7] Such a strategy, derived from Colin Rowe's idea of contextualism, is relatively detached from references to specific, iconic imagery that appear in the work of Rossi, for example.

Infill does not necessarily suggest considering 'the new beside the historic' and their problematic implications, although such considerations could be part of it. The focus instead is on the disjunction that could potentially occur when the new comes into existence alongside the pre-existing. Much of the criticism of contemporary architecture and planning arises from both the problematic autonomy from, and the overly cautious subservience to, the existing context.

050   Enis Aldallal | Site and Composition: Design strategies
Husam AlWaer and | in architecture and urbanism
Soumyen Bandyopadhyay

Site-by-site relationships are inspired by their physical as well as cultural contexts; their success can be determined by the degree to which they effectively address the reciprocity between city artefacts. In that sense it parallels Wright's notion of completing the landscape with a building, since both of them – the building and the circumstance – are perceived in continuity, i.e. producing architecture as a stylised contextual fill.[8] The circumstance stimulates the sentiments of the architect's sense of place, who attempts to produce harmonic designs that, in turn, endeavour for integrity and perceptual wholeness. Bernard Tschumi suggested design strategies that architects may use when faced with an 'urban infill' problem:

- Design a masterly construction, an inspired architectural gesture (a composition).

- Take what exists, fill in the gaps, complete the text, and scribble in the margins (a complement).

- Deconstruct what exists by critically analyzing the historical layers that precede it, even adding other layers derived from elsewhere – from other cities, other parks (a palimpsest).

- Search for an intermediary – an abstract system to mediate between the site (as well as all given constraints) and some other concept, beyond city or program (a mediation).[9]

Such general strategies should soon evolve into proposals based on an architect's interpretation of an existing context and underpin decisions to intervene within that context.[10] Given the rarity with which the opportunity of designing the iconic object building presents itself and the problematic nature of its wider application, the urban infill is an inevitability the architect needs to engage with. This, however, is not easy to achieve; while anticipating continuity of overt or latent morphological

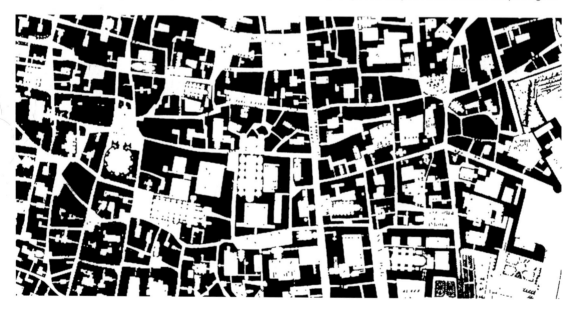

Figure 3.1 Map of Rome, Giambattista Nolli, 1748 (after Trancik, R., 1986 *Finding Lost Space*).

patterns, the architect should also be aware of the need for the reordering of fragments as a reflection of ordering the world. To diagnose the level of 'spatial' coherence of sites, to frame their entire image into a comprehensible relationship with their settings, and to test their formal qualities, two representational modes – but also analytical mechanisms – need to be examined: the figure–ground paradigm, and sectional analysis.

Figure–ground

The two-dimensional coherence of sites – in plan – could be examined through the figure–ground paradigm. Exemplified by the drawings of the 'Greek Vase' (see Chapter 1), this paradigm is one of the most common graphical methods that is employed to illustrate a building within its wider context. A drawing that summarises buildings and their in-between voids into black-and-white graphical representation, the figure–ground paradigm has been used by architects and planners to evaluate the qualities of the compositional coherence – of inner and outer spaces – based on geometry. It was also used for identifying the characteristics of the interstices between city artefacts, that is the building coverage portrayed with the mass/void relationship.[11] Its early emergence was through the map of Rome prepared by Giambattista Nolli (1748; Figure 3.1).

Although the black figures are actually the only thing drawn on the white background, the resulting white voids are what give meaning and existence to the black figures, highlighting interrelation between the two.[12] In that sense, the reciprocal relationship between the black figures and the white voids is what determines their consistency towards achieving coherent relationship or meaningful pattern. In the latter half of the twentieth century, Colin Rowe re-employed this paradigm which emerged as an iconic anchor through its highlighting 'relationships rather than objects, pattern rather than picture',[13] and inclusion rather than exclusion, to reveal what was impossible to achieve by means of other methods. In the 1980s, Roger

Trancik adopted this technique alongside 'linkage theory' and 'place theory' to find lost spaces between urban sites.[14] Its planimetric importance in establishing connectivity will be discussed further in Chapter 4.

The focus, then, is not on establishing a framework for producing a universal, geometrical system of connections[15] that would control the entire body of towns or cities through master planning. Instead, the purpose is to use the figure–ground paradigm geometrically to mediate between the adjacent artefacts of a specific place and to produce an integrated quality and sense of enclosure. Through the use of geometrical configuration in the broadest sense, this integrated approach proposes to achieve the uninterrupted mesh of activities within urban passageways and interstitial spaces, and the fusion of the indoor and the outdoor.[16] The differentiation between the indoor and the outdoor is defined by an in-between event, which is 'conceived as a positive entity in an integrated relationship with surrounding solids'.[17] The articulation of the public and the private differentiates the civic buildings from urban voids and brings the public into clarified relationship with the private. Its mission therefore is 'to clarify the structure of urban spaces in a city or a district by establishing a hierarchy of spaces of different sizes that are individually enclosed but ordered directionally in relation to each other'.[18] The use of the figure–ground paradigm as a design strategy in site practices not only pays attention to the built and the inbuilt, the private and the public, and the interior and the exterior spaces, but also allows the designer to better perceive the impact of new interventions. The articulation and understanding of a more complete urban topography related to individual sites could help organise our built environment better.[19]

The intention is to move away from a universal understanding of a site's relationship with its surroundings – a figure that relates to the wider networks of the city and its organisational patterns in a predictable and reproducible manner. The intention is neither to idealise site situation

052 Enis Aldallal | Site and Composition: Design strategies
Husam AlWaer and | in architecture and urbanism
Soumyen Bandyopadhyay |

nor to obliterate its identity. Considering site as ideal circumstance 'removes site matters from design process'; thus 'it negates the meaning of site as a particular location'.[20] Acknowledging the existing conditions or patterns of a specific location does not mean that a proposed scheme should literally re-employ extant materials or be spatially continuous, or identical in form or planning. Instead, as James Stirling's Civic Centre Competition for Derby (1970; Figure 3.2) illustrates, the intervention should aim to accommodate *performances* similar to that of the existing.[21]

Site fragments: the Wexner Centre for the Visual Arts

The reading of the Wexner Centre simultaneously as a fragment of a larger site or as a site that comprises fragments highlights its contradictory nature. However, the difference between these two readings contributes to conceptualising the architectural object either as a site-making approach or as single-building approach. The site-making approach gives equal value to each fragment or element of site – both the existing and the proposed. In the single-building approach, the site is most often considered as a self-contained fragment that creates its own narratives.

Peter Eisenman's Wexner Centre for the Visual Arts (1989) in Columbus, Ohio could be perceived through this specific lens. Its position between two major entities – the city and the university campus – highlights its mediating role between two differing event settings at widely differing scales. Through its geometry, the Wexner integrates the geometries of these polar entities too, as it 'projects an image of belonging both to the campus and to the larger context of Ohio'.[22] Eisenman's proposal was the first choice among the shortlisted projects as it addressed the possibility of achieving a better connection between the oval of the campus and the city (Figures 3.3–3.5).[23] The task of integrating the site with its context was achieved through 'historical references and a grid structure resulting from the overlay of university and community mapping strategies' (Figure 3.6).[24] In response to programmatic

Figure 3.2 Competition entry of the Civic Centre; Derby, James Stirling (after Hays, M., ed., 1998 *Oppositions Reader*).

Figure 3.3 Peter Eisenman. The Wexner Centre for the Visual Arts, Ohio State University, Columbus, Ohio: city–site axis, looking westward.

demands, the Wexner also integrates two pre-existing fragments on site: the Mershon Auditorium and the Weigel Hall. Instrumental moves play significant roles in achieving connections between the building, the site, its immediate context, the city and beyond. The design idea of this building is centred on the grid, which appeared as the key compositional element down to the smallest detailing of the building. The grid was a metaphorical allusion to the history of the planning of American cities but also to the conquest of the New Continent in general. In so doing, the site of the Wexner as a fragment has played a mediating role between entities that extend beyond their physical extent in their true cultural value and significance, introducing a wholeness that transcends tangible space and time.

This idea was strengthened on a more immediate social and urban level by the links established through the north–south and the east–west axes of the project with the streets surrounding the site. The sense of unity was achieved through growing clarity as one moved from outside into the interior and the walkways of the site.[25] The architecture and the programme at Wexner are grounded in 'a belief that the ultimate concerns of art and expression lie in the social domains of economics, politics, and history rather than in the narrowly defined records of aesthetics and styles rehearsed in art or architecture texts'.[26] Chapter 4 will further investigate the Wexner to clarify the role of each of its fragments in the process of site making.

Figure 3.4 The Wexner Centre: site–campus axis, view from the east.

054   Enis Aldallal | Site and Composition: Design strategies
Husam AlWaer and | in architecture and urbanism
Soumyen Bandyopadhyay |

Figure 3.5 The Wexner Centre: campus–site axis, looking eastward.

Utilising fragments – the grid-scaffold – to refer to the distant surroundings is not a new idea at the Wexner, as such initiatives date back to the nineteenth century.[27] Here, however, its significance lies in the way in which Eisenman privileged it for 'site-making' rather than for 'building'. Thus, the significance of the Wexner is in the use of cultural and geometrical methods of interpretation and construction which 'altered and informed how a site fragment was found, defined, and valued, and then how that fragment was grafted onto a designed landscape'.[28] The process of exploring, defining and evaluating this fragment is what distinguishes Eisenman's work from that of his contemporaries. Some critics have read the Wexner as a building that was never completed, principally due to the dramatic intervention of the intersected, white grid-scaffold. Kay Jones argues that 'there is no habitable,

dominant interior place which harmoniously shelters while it orients the inhabitant to the organization of the building's spaces'.[29] She also argues that the intersected grid has isolated the Wexner's main lobby from other facilities – the galleries, café, black box, the book shop and the theatre, all located on the lower floor. 'What remains', she contends, 'above ground is a non-building. Some portions of the built mass contain nothing.'[30] Jones' argument is correct when we read the site and the building as an autonomous, isolated occurrence. The intention at the Wexner, as Eisenman himself stated, 'was not to make yet another object-shelter enclosure as a dominant value'.[31] Jones' contention – that the Wexner had its head cut from its body through the superimposition of the grid – could also be viewed as what Tschumi terms the 'in-between',[32] as significant as the constituent fragments themselves. For there are always

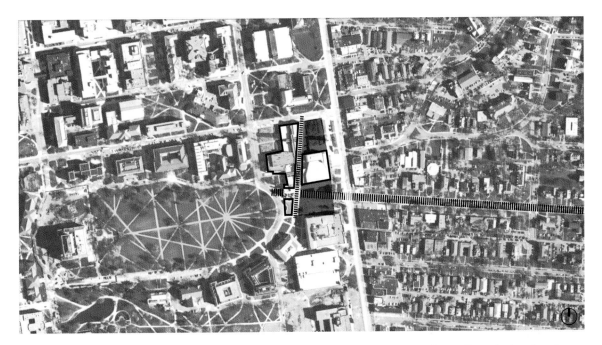

Figure 3.6 The Wexner Centre: diagram illustrating how the urban axes fragment the building.

splits between fragments and those splits have no function other than being the connector or passage between one fragment and another.[33] At the town hall in Saynatsalo, Alvar Aalto's understanding of composition led him to evaluate and employ the fragment as an order as well as a social construct. On Aalto's perception of fragments, Roger Connah suggests that:

> [t]o an architect like Aalto they encouraged an altered historicist totality, something patched up, bandaged, synthesized expressively after decomposition had taken place.… This became Aalto's so called reconciliation of oppositions.… An order, a fragment of order at once identifiable as humanist and synthetic, historicist and expressive; a reconciled union.[34]

A more fundamental conflict appears to be at the heart of the Wexner project: '[i]t is the sustained clash between the high modern desire for isolation and pure form – the building as a sculpture – and the postmodern obligation to relevance and context'.[35] The architecture of this centre could thus be regarded as a postmodern unearthing of practices that modernism disregarded in its amnesia. modernist practices – at the root of Eisenman's early explorations (see Chapter 1) – however, are re-evaluated, tempered and redeployed, serving as a constant reminder of the building's tantalising poise between abstraction and materialisation, and between semiotics and poetics.

The problematic engagement with site matters emerges as a result of dealing with the site in a myopic and exclusive manner: as an abstract, aesthetic geometrical entity, an exaggerated scientific phenomenon, an object of

056   Enis Aldallal | Site and Composition: Design strategies
Husam AlWaer and | in architecture and urbanism
Soumyen Bandyopadhyay |

historiographical interest,[36] or as a nostalgic perception of it as a bounded – emancipated – plot.[37] Each of those instances also points towards the strong correspondence present between the site and its surrounding, which in turn draws our attention to the phenomenon of 'urban infill'.

Sectional analysis

The compositional extension to the figure–ground paradigm is the vertical articulation of the figure against its ground. The section as a design tool is of great importance to complete the investigation initiated by plan in terms of comprehending the configuration of site-by-site relationship. To acknowledge the physical context of an urban site is to bring some of its fundamental characteristics into the new design by means of mediation. Translational shifts could be useful even to mediate between extremely divergent urban conditions.[38]

Translational – not literal – shifts are what Le Corbusier employed at the house/studio Atelier Ozenfant (1922), which responded subtly to the particularity of the patterns found within the neighbourhood (Figure 3.7).[39] Wendy Redfield

Figure 3.7 Le Corbusier. Atelier Ozenfant, Paris: view of the front facade and longitudinal section (section after Burns & Kahn, eds, 2005 *Site Matters*).

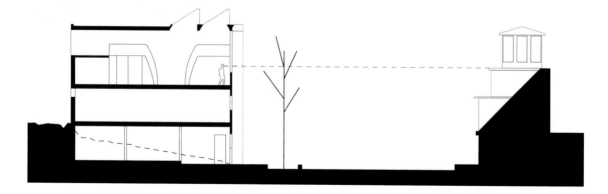

illustrated this by a longitudinal section taken through the building to reveal a 'startling transition in site circumstances from back to front',[40] a transition that starts compressed and straight at the back – where the Hopital Universite de Paris across Rue du Square Montsouris is located – to open up towards the front – where the monumental reservoir across Avenue Reille is present, and where the urban density is low and the horizon is much more tangible and clearly evident. Redfield observed that the studio level aligned precisely with the top of the reservoir wall, 'bringing the two – the studio and the reservoir – into a direct, even parallel relationship'.[41] Through the mediating Atelier Ozenfant, Le Corbusier managed to make a graceful transition from

the monumental character of Avenue Reille to the small, pedestrian Rue du Square Montsouris.[42] As a result, both the studio and the reservoir equally share their geometries in a way that makes them belong to the civic context of Paris.

Le Corbusier was grappling with the problem of mediating within the urban topography; but what if the architect was confronted with the need to engage with both urban and natural topographies at the same time? Eisenman's Aronoff Centre for the Arts at the University of Cincinnati (1996) engages with such a problem (Figure 3.8). Through a painstaking process Peter Eisenman produces a complex intervention that, on one hand, 'allows differentiating

Figure 3.8 Peter Eisenman. Aronoff Centre for the Arts, University of Cincinnati, Cincinnati, Ohio: location between the 'natural' and the urban topographies.

058　　Enis Aldallal | Site and Composition: Design strategies
　　Husam AlWaer and | in architecture and urbanism
　　Soumyen Bandyopadhyay |

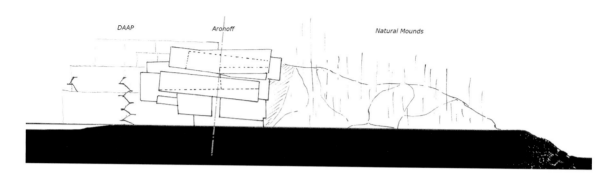

Figure 3.9 Aronoff Centre: conceptual sketch – between the 'natural' and the urban topographies.

the old and the new buildings to become blurred'[43] and, on the other, relates the building to its natural setting. It is worth mentioning that the process employed at the Aronoff combined the use of the sectional tool alongside planimetric configuration. In section, the new addition proposed a set of boxes morphed through a series of torques affecting their north side (Figure 3.9). However, in order to establish the diagram in section, a relationship between the boxes of the Aronoff and the floor slabs of the existing College of Design, Architecture, Art and Planning (DAAP) had to be determined. This, in turn, necessitated defining a practical response to the reality of construction and the simultaneous maintenance of the overriding formal logic in section.[44]

The mediating role the Aronoff played on site was through its developed vocabulary, which 'came from the curves of land forms and the chevron forms of the existing building setting up a dynamic relationship to organize the space between the two'.[45] Twisting the boxes, spatially, at the mound side, was in fact a response to the natural topography that the architect noted; that in turn made the columns vertical on the DAAP side and sloped on the mound side, 'with profile of the building's geometry'.[46] The existing DAAP buildings allowed the addition to have its own separate levels, floor-to-floor heights and connecting stairs,[47] resulting in non-aligned floors throughout the

buildings except for 'Level 500' in the Aronoff, which formed the only common floor level across the two buildings.

As a result, 'any traditional section that could be cut and drawn would be orthogonal to only one box in the wireframe'[48] and the sectional drawing did not necessarily help in providing accurate information towards its physical build process.[49] The focus was on creating a response to the context, as Eisenman mentions: 'Our idea in the design process was to have the building develop from within the place itself – the site, the existing building, and the spirit of the college.'[50] From the composite process of development the building went through, it becomes difficult to distinguish the pre-existing buildings from the new. Figures 3.10–3.12 illustrate the step-by-step process of torques applied to the main boxes forming the main body of the Aronoff Centre, to reconcile the new intervention with the existing urban components and the surrounding nature.

What Eisenman suggested at the Aronoff was more than a conventional contextualist approach to architecture, quite unlike interventions that merely retain or update the proportions and formal languages of the existing. Further, 'in the Aronoff Centre the visual relation to the referent is always confounded', making the resulting 'forms, spaces, sections, and plans … [not to] resemble the pre-existing buildings'.[51] The addition follows the bends and turns of

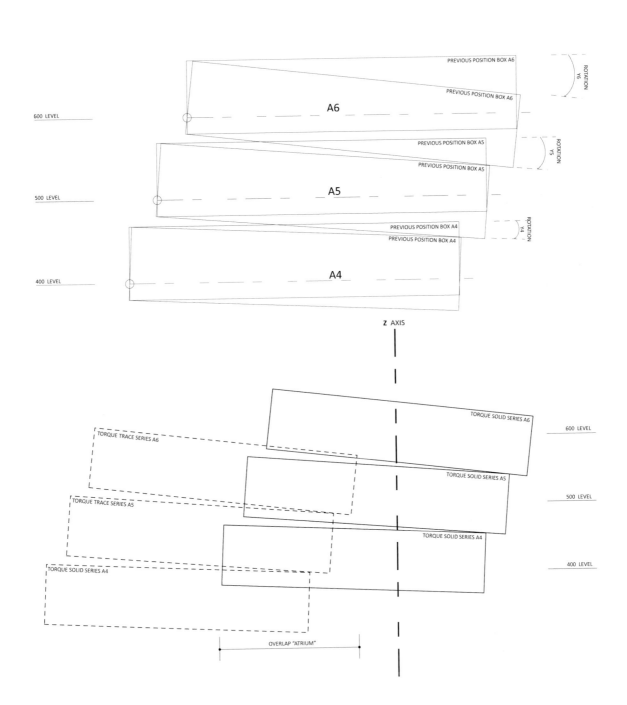

PREVIOUS POSITION BOX A6

PREVIOUS POSITION BOX A6

ROTATION Y6

A6

600 LEVEL

PREVIOUS POSITION BOX A5

PREVIOUS POSITION BOX A5

ROTATION Y5

A5

500 LEVEL

PREVIOUS POSITION BOX A4

PREVIOUS POSITION BOX A4

ROTATION Y4

A4

400 LEVEL

Z AXIS

TORQUE SOLID SERIES A6

600 LEVEL

TORQUE TRACE SERIES A6

TORQUE SOLID SERIES A5

500 LEVEL

TORQUE TRACE SERIES A5

TORQUE SOLID SERIES A4

400 LEVEL

TORQUE SOLID SERIES A4

OVERLAP "ATRIUM"

060   Enis Aldallal | Site and Composition: Design strategies
Husam AlWaer and | in architecture and urbanism
Soumyen Bandyopadhyay |

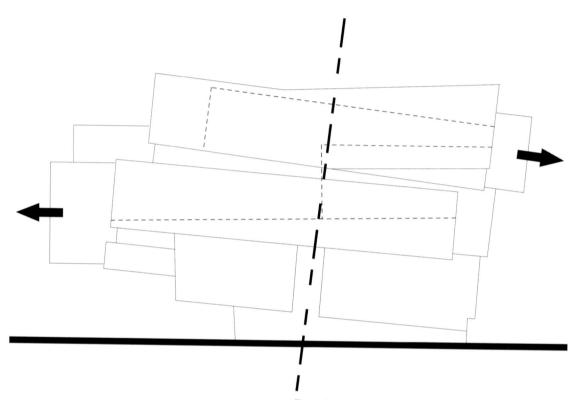

Figures 3.10–3.12 Aronoff Centre: the series of overlays and torques applied to the boxes to define sectional configuration (after Davidson, C., ed., *Eleven Authors in Search of a Building*).

the existing buildings as well as the natural contours of the encompassing topography, leaving a gap for the observer to perceive how the disjunctions and connections were actually accomplished. What the Aronoff endeavoured to achieve was its role as a positive fragment that aimed for 'completion on a higher level of synthesis and perfection'.[52] The building crucially highlights the role of boundaries that interrelate two entities rather than segregating them.

Boundary as communicative space

A boundary is a line or a thing that indicates a border or limit – something that marks the outside edge or the limits of a spatial unit. Boundaries are also employed to establish private and public ownership by determining the exact location where one piece of land is distinguishable from another. The boundary has the power to include or to exclude. In understanding wholeness it must be emphasised that the fragment would not be a fragment without the existence of wholeness.[53] Nothing exists in isolation, as Ellin notes, 'only in relation (or context), whether it is a building, a city, or a person'.[54] However, many attempts to restore that wholeness have resulted in failures, as architecture has sought to collaborate with sculpture or painting, and with landscape architecture and urbanism.[55] In all of these disciplines – which often have relied primarily on the visual qualities of the fragment – the role of mediation in linking fragments has remained limited and therefore has managed to achieve only a partial wholeness. Even the smallest fragments in a system – and buildings are certainly not the smallest – have the potential to relate to each other through their relationship to other fragments. What needs to be emphasised here is that the boundaries are the entities where the relationships between fragments manifest themselves. As Tschumi reminds us, even the clash between fragments is a relationship, where 'it is not the clash … that counts but the movements between them'.[56]

Heidegger considered the boundary as 'not that at which something stops but … that from which something begins its presencing'.[57] The in-between circumstance is an instrument facilitating passage or mediation between one event and another, like those elaborated at the Wexner Centre; its significance lies in the fact that it is as vital as the fragments themselves in the process of composition. As Vesely observed, 'the subject matter consists … of the relationship between these objects and between the object and the intervening space',[58] in which the objects are like fragments of sentences held between quotation marks, and '[y]et they are not quotations. They simply melt into the work.'[59] Vesely has described this in-between circumstance as the *communicative space*;[60] the meaning of communicative movements – between individual fragments – is reliant on their quality and on their reference to the pre-existing world. The fragmentary nature of representation is revealed through dialogue with the concrete reality of space.[61] The palpable structure of that space is the result of a process in which the relations between fragments, figures and architectures 'create a series of possible settings that may eventually be translated into a publishable configuration'.[62] To identify this configuration in art, architecture and urbanism one needs to dismantle the strained or closed boundaries that often characterise the rigid disciplinary identities, hierarchies and their stratifications[63] of mundane constitutions to accept constructive dialogues between different disciplines and at different scales of operation.

In expressing the encompassing world, a painter's colour arrangement must also carry with it the expression of the invisible whole, or else the picture will only hint at fragments but not provide them with the sense of unity.[64] Each brushstroke (fragment) must perform certain pictorial roles to merge into the space it is employed within – either in the middle of an object or on its perimeter (boundary). Each stroke must, in addition, contain the atmosphere, the composition, the character, the outline and the style of the adjacent.[65] Thus, regardless of where the fragment is situated it has to mediate the new circumstance in order for it to avoid a mere symbolic juxtaposition. This mediation comes through the boundaries it shares with other fragments, i.e. through the common boundaries the characteristics of the surrounding circumstances could be brought into the fragment. In fact, what determines coherence is both the subject and the communicative space, the latter always awaiting elaboration. It is the space that defines the relationships between objects. Articulation of that space is often difficult to achieve, certainly in painting, as the Cubist Georges Braque once described: 'it seems to me just as difficult to paint the space "between" as the things themselves'.[66] Despite its hard brush strokes, the *Ai bordi dell'acqua* painting reveals a high sensitivity of the fragments – brush strokes – towards the boundary, especially within the space separating the water vacuum from that of the ground. It is the boundaries that manifest unity as they are the passages between the variety of fragments of colour, scale, thinness and thickness.

In architecture the idea of boundary – as space – is further complicated as it has to deal with the communicative space as something material and experiential, as something that accounts for the unity or disunity of the constituent objects as well as human actions. It is important to point out that the idea of boundary expressed here is not about the physical perimeter or the property line of site that bounds it from other artefacts.[67] Rather, it is the in-between space defined by the proximity of adjacent fragments, events or sites. The continuity of communicative movements

062   Enis Aldallal | Site and Composition: Design strategies
    Husam AlWaer and | in architecture and urbanism
    Soumyen Bandyopadhyay |

between isolated fragments or between interiority and exteriority of an architectural setting, however, manifests itself in the same way as in painting.[68] In architecture the interrelations between two architectural fragments more usually take place through communicative boundaries as positive spaces,[69] that is through spaces 'ruled by the situational structure of typical elements'.[70] Without such spaces or boundaries, elements could not be connected or interrelated; these are spaces that are not negative but active material entities, as Kay Jones had indicated regarding the scaffold grid passageways at the Wexner.

In intervening within an urban context, such boundaries would require reactivation and rearticulation in order to strengthen the sense of integration between the constituent parts (the existing and the infill). Thus the boundaries are the spaces where the exteriors of buildings interact, but they are also the definitive elements through which the exterior and the interior spaces meet (see Chapter 5). While the first directs our focus towards the urbanistic aspect of architecture, the second extends this sequence of events inwards – but also outwards – towards achieving cohesion between the city and the most interior of architectural spaces.[71] Blurring the boundaries between the architecture and the outside by creating mediating spaces

can be exemplified by Wright's Robie House in Chicago, Illinois (1906), where the movement from the 'public' to the 'private' to the 'particular' has been carefully articulated, both in plan and in section (Figures 3.13–3.14). Wright set up a sequence of interstices and pockets from the walkway outside to the terrace of the living room on the second floor. This has been spatially reinforced by the cantilevered roofs of the terraces that permeate the public and the private to manifest spatial fusion.

Eisenman has managed to create a communicative space between the new and the pre-existing at the Aronoff Centre; the acknowledgement of the chevron configuration has contributed to the melding of the pre-existing and the proposed plans into one coherent spatial order. The process strengthened the meeting of the existing and the intervention, creating a common space connecting the Aronoff, the DAAP and even the exterior, fusing these entities into a wholeness (Figures 3.15–3.16).[72] This resulted in blurring the distinguishing boundaries of the two entities, which found a compromising – communicative – space to meet. The external spaces at the main entrance of the Aronoff act as thresholds and interstices that negotiate the meeting of the public event of the campus and the private one of the Aronoff's interior.

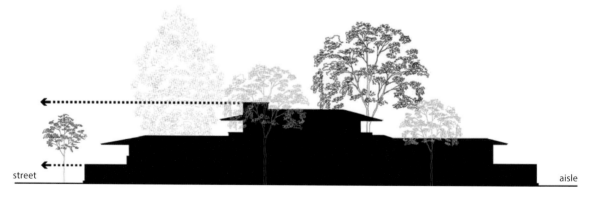

street   aisle

Figure 3.13 Frank L. Wright. Robie House, Chicago, Illinois: the communicative space of the house defined between the two arrows (after Hoffmann, D., 1984, *Frank Lloyd Wright's Robie House*).

Figure 3.14 Robie House: communicative space defined by the overhanging roof of the living room.

Within the city, boundaries are significantly more complex in their perception and less clearly discernible. Spaces between buildings are charged with connective energy, the intensity of which varies according to the nature of, and relationship between, buildings (Figure 3.17).[73] Each interstitial space is 'a space of specific scale determined by the size of the gathering it can contain, and by the height, character and design of its boundaries'.[74] Articulating 'the differentiation of solids and voids' is what constitutes the fabric of the city and establishes the physical sequences and visual orientation within.[75] Their oft-understood value as voids is a problematic one as such a perception is underscored by the understanding that buildings are the only positive spatial entities. It is a wisdom received

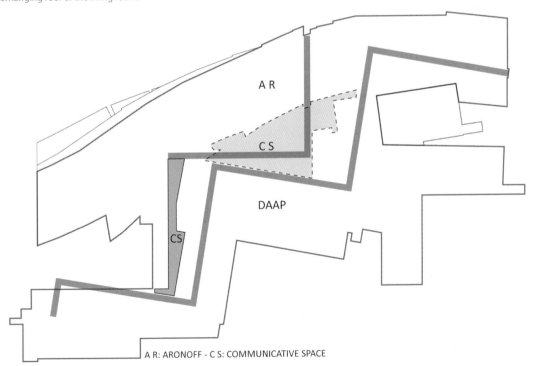

A R: ARONOFF - C S: COMMUNICATIVE SPACE

Figure 3.15 Aronoff Centre: 3. Level +400 plan showing the communicative spaces, CS (after Davidson, C., ed., *Eleven Authors in Search of a Building*).

064   Enis Aldallal │ Site and Composition: Design strategies
Husam AlWaer and │ in architecture and urbanism
Soumyen Bandyopadhyay │

Figure 3.16 Aronoff Centre: inside the communicative space.

from a misconceived idea of location that disregards spatial continuity,[76] removing the opportunity for the city to become greater than the sum of its fragmentary parts.[77] Treating the site as an isolated fragment, powered by the instrumental aesthetic, scientific and even historic approaches defining its relationship to the surroundings, perpetuates its isolation and amorphousness. It is the spaces between architectures that give life to architecture.

Trancik has emphasised the need for articulating the perimeters of city blocks to establish 'outdoor rooms

containing corners, niches, pockets, and corridors',[78] while Ellin, following a similar path, has advocated treating urban artefacts as interactive, translucent fragments to create *urban porosity*, which through its 'permeable membranes is able to separate and unite buildings from and with the surrounding physical and cultural landscape'.[79] In that sense, boundaries are 'important validators, identity makers, and thresholds' at the core of relationships between city artefacts and their inhabitants,[80] allowing divergent scales of inflection on fragments, as well as on the whole.

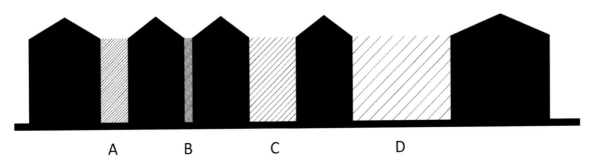

A   B   C   D

Figure 3.17 In-between urban spaces represented in different densities of shading.

Conclusion: site at different scales of integrity and fragmentation

Consistent reiteration of wholeness is fundamental to the sustenance of the built environment; relationships are the driving forces behind the built environment we inhabit. While the existence of fragmentation is inevitable and perhaps even desirable, it is important, as this chapter highlights, to treat sites as positive fragments, capable of conjoining into active wholeness. The whole is much more than the sum of its parts, which requires not only focusing on every fragment, but on understanding deeper, underlying patterns of relationships between parts.

By the dawn of the twentieth century, as a result of the demanding modern lifestyle, the development of new representational methods in certain spheres of the visual arts – especially in painting and sculpture – had also catapulted into architecture. The struggle was to find novel and appropriate methods of representing the architectural object as a reflection of emerging modern socio-cultural tendencies and concomitant world of the everyday. In both art and architecture fragmented ways of thinking about modernism resulted in fragmented modes and methods of production and the increasing – often unintended – erection of disciplinary boundaries. The most demanding part of any collaboration – especially involving architects and artists – will have been 'the transition from the conceptual or

design stage to implementation. This seems to be the point at which there is most likely to be conflict over definition of roles, authorship and responsibility.'[81] Because the majority of the modern movement architects understood architecture either as a technological problem or as a piece of pure artwork, the modern city could not, unfortunately, escape a collective, accretive quality. As a result, the wholeness they sought failed to overcome the negative aspects of fragmentation in order to restore the unity and coherence of the architectural object and its setting.

The physical fragmentation occurring between city artefacts is not due to their divergent typologies – as cities have always sustained diverse activities and accommodated many building types. It is because of the problematic way in which the term 'site' was approached – as a mere bounded, self-contained entity, which ignored the notion of boundaries as the critical communicative element that connected – not segregated – these urban fragments. We need to think of fragments as positive entities that carry the promise of performing and contributing towards the preferred wholeness. We often conceive and design buildings as objects separated from use and context. This separation has 'led to the illusion that the world is actually constituted of separate fragments and … this will cause us to act in such a way that we in fact produce the very fragmentation implied in our attitude to the theory'.[82] As suggested, the Wexner Centre should indeed be read as a

066   Enis Aldallal | Site and Composition: Design strategies
Husam AlWaer and | in architecture and urbanism
Soumyen Bandyopadhyay |

fragment of a greater whole within a larger context, which 'relates again the scope of city planning as a means of increasing the unity of the complex whole … the building which is a whole at one level and a fragment of a greater whole at another level'.[83]

The disjunction manifested through the consideration of fragmentation as a negative phenomenon lies in the consistent ignoring of the idea and nature of boundaries. This chapter has highlighted the importance of the edge being as important and effective as the subject matter itself and has identified it as an entity whose role is to interrelate the architectural objects.[84] Through these boundaries our comprehension extends into bigger totalities that enclose the smaller, more immediate ones. For, 'some pattern of connections will be laid upon the earth within those boundaries. Generally producing a set of inner edges upon which our comprehension of the place depends'.[85] From art, to architecture, and to urbanism, the positive role of boundaries has the same power in images as it has in city spaces,[86] enabling a better perception towards building a coherent built environment.

Notes

1 Rossi, A., *The Architecture of the City*, Cambridge, MA: MIT Press, 1984, p. 21.

2 www.patrikschumacher.com/Texts/morality1.htm, accessed 30 March 2015.

3 Ellin, N., *Integral Urbanism*, New York and London: Routledge, 2006, p. 17.

4 Leatherbarrow, D., *Topographical Stories: Studies in Landscape and Architecture*, Pennsylvania: University of Pennsylvania Press, 2004.

5 Meyer, E., 'Site Citations', in Burns, C. & Kahn, A. (eds), *Site Matters: Design Concepts, Histories and Strategies*, New York and Abingdon: Routledge, 2005, p. 115.

6 Smith, P., *The Dynamics of Urbanism*, London: Hutchinson, 1974, p. 72.

7 Cohen, S., 'Physical Context/Cultural Context: Including it All', in Hays, M. (ed.), *Oppositions Reader: Selected Readings from a Journal for Ideas and Criticism in Architecture 1973–1984*, New York: Princeton Architectural Press, 1998, p. 67.

8 Leatherbarrow, D., *The Roots of Architectural Invention*, Cambridge: Cambridge University Press, 1993, p. 21.

9 Tschumi, B., *Architecture and Disjunction*, Cambridge, MA: MIT Press, 1996, pp. 191–192.

10 Isenstadt, S., 'Contested Context', in Burns, C. & Kahn, A. (eds), *Site Matters: Design Concepts, Histories and Strategies*, New York and Abingdon: Routledge, 2005, p. 158.

11 Trancik, R., *Finding Lost Space*, New York: Van Nostrand Reinhold, 1986, p. 97.

12 Dripps, R., 'Ground Work', in Burns, C. & Kahn, A. (eds), *Site Matters: Design Concepts, Histories and Strategies*, New York and Abingdon: Routledge, 2005, p.73.

13 Ellis, W., 'Type and Context in Urbanism: Colin Rowe's Contextualism', in Hays, M. (ed.), *Oppositions Reader: Selected Readings from a Journal for Ideas and Criticism in Architecture 1973–1984*, New York: Princeton Architectural Press, 1998, p. 231.

14 Trancik, op. cit., p. 97.

15 Salingaros, N., 'Complexity of Urban Coherence', *Journal of Urban Design* 5(3), 2000, p. 291.

16 Ellin, op. cit., p. 53.

17 Trancik, op. cit., p. 98.

18 Ibid., p. 97.

19 See, for example, Talen, E., 'Evaluating Good Urban Form in an Inner-city Neighbourhood: An Empirical Application', *Journal of Architectural and Planning Research* 22(3), 2005, p. 208.

20 Redfield, W., 'The Suppressed Site', in Burns, C. & Kahn, A. (eds), *Site Matters: Design Concepts, Histories and Strategies*, New York and Abingdon: Routledge, 2005, p.185.

21 Leatherbarrow, D., *Uncommon Ground: Architecture, Technology and Topography*, Cambridge, MA: MIT Press, 2002, p. 183.

22 Davidson, C., *Tracing Eisenman*, New York: Thames & Hudson, 2006, p. 112.

23 Moneo, R., *Theoretical Anxiety and Design Strategies in the Work of Eight Contemporary Architects*, Cambridge, MA: MIT Press, 2004, p. 180.

24 Stearns, R., 'Building as Catalyst', in Moneo, R. & Vidler, A. (eds), *Wexner Centre for the Visual Arts, the Ohio State University*, New York: Rizzoli, 1989, p. 24.

25 Green, J., 'Algorithms for Discovery', in Moneo, R. & Vidler, A. (eds), *Wexner Centre for the Visual Arts, the Ohio State University*, New York: Rizzoli, 1989, p. 30.

26 Ibid., p. 28.

27 Meyer, op. cit., p. 108.

28 Ibid.

29 Jones, K., 'The Wexner Fragments for the Visual Arts', *Journal of Architectural Education* 43(3), 1990, p. 34.

30 Ibid.

31 Ibid.

32 Tschumi, op. cit., p. 95.

33 Ibid.

34 Connah, R., *Writing Architecture: Fantômas Fragments Fictions – An Architectural Journey Through the Twentieth Century*, Cambridge, MA: MIT Press, 1989, p. 32.

35 Green, op. cit., p. 30.

068   Enis Aldallal | Site and Composition: Design strategies
Husam AlWaer and | in architecture and urbanism
Soumyen Bandyopadhyay |

36 Burns, C. & Kahn, A., 'Introduction', in Burns, C. & Kahn, A. (eds), *Site Matters: Design Concepts, Histories and Strategies*, New York and Abingdon: Routledge, 2005, p. xv.

37 Hogue, M., 'The Site as a Project: Lessons from Land Art and Conceptual Art', *Journal of Architectural Education* 57(3), 2004, p. 54.

38 Redfield, op. cit., p. 194.

39 Ibid., p. 193.

40 Ibid., p. 194.

41 Ibid., p. 196.

42 Ibid., p. 197.

43 Barry, D., 'Connecting the Dots: The Dimensions of a Wire Frame', in Davidson, C. (ed.), *Eleven Authors in Search of a Building*, New York: Monacelli, 1996, p. 49.

44 Ibid., p. 51.

45 Ibid.

46 Ibid., p. 57.

47 Ibid., p. 54.

48 Ibid., p. 58.

49 Ibid., p. 58.

50 Whiting, S., 'Building Inside Out', in Davidson, C. (ed.), *Eleven Authors in Search of a Building*, New York: Monacelli, 1996, pp. 101–102.

51 Kolbowski, S., 'Fringe Benefits', in Davidson, C. (ed.), *Eleven Authors in Search of a Building*, New York: Monacelli, 1996, p. 135.

52 Vesely, D., *Architecture in the Age of Divided Representation: The Question of Creativity in the Shadow of Production*, Cambridge, MA: MIT Press, 2004, pp. 332–333.

53 Ibid., p. 331.

54 Ellin, op. cit., p. 83.

55 Ibid.

56 Tschumi, op. cit., p. 95.

57 Sharr, A., *Thinkers for Architects: Heidegger for Architects*, New York: Routledge, 2007, p. 51.

58 Vesely, op. cit., pp. 332–338.

59 Tschumi, op. cit., p. 95.

60 Vesely, op. cit., p. 345.

61 Ibid., p. 346.

62 Ibid., p. 349.

63 Ellin, op. cit., p. 84.

64 Vesely, op. cit., pp. 335–336.

65 Ibid., p. 336.

66 Ibid.

67 Beauregard, R., 'From Place to Site', in Burns, C. & Kahn, A. (eds), *Site Matters: Design Concepts, Histories and Strategies*, New York and Abingdon: Routledge, 2005, p. 39.

68 Vesely, op. cit., p. 345.

69 Smith, P., *Architecture and the Principle of Harmony*, London: RIBA, 1987, p. 111.

70 Vesely, op. cit., p. 345.

71 Trancik, op. cit., p. 100.

72 Barry, op. cit., p. 54.

73 Smith, *Architecture and the Principle of Harmony*, p. 111.

74 Trancik, op. cit., p. 100.

75 Ibid.

76 Sharr, op. cit., p. 51.

77 Ellin, op. cit., p. 82.

78 Trancik, op. cit., p. 100.

79 Ellin, op. cit., pp. 76–77.

80 Ibid., p. 91.

81 Melhuish, C., 'Art and Architecture: The Dynamics of Collaboration', in Trasi, N. (ed.), *Interdisciplinary Architecture*, London: Wiley Academy, 2001, p. 26.

82 Bohm, D., *Wholeness and the Implicate Order*, London and New York: Routledge, 2012 (reprint), quoted in Franck, K. & Lepori, B., *Architecture from the Inside Out: From the Body, the Senses, the Site, and the Community*, London: Wiley Academy, 2007, p. 165.

83 Venturi, op. cit., p. 102.

84 See, Bloomer, K. & Moore, C., 'Body, Memory, and Architecture', in Jencks, C. & Kropf, K. (eds) *Theories and Manifestoes of Contemporary Architecture*, London: Wiley Academy, 2006 (second edition), p. 72.

85 Ibid.

86 Vesely, op. cit., p. 343.

4 The planimetric composition of site

074   Enis Aldallal | Site and Composition: Design strategies
Husam AlWaer and | in architecture and urbanism
Soumyen Bandyopadhyay |

CONNOTATIVE MODE	REPRESENTATIONAL MODE	REPRESENTATIONAL TOOL
MEMORY	PLACE	
PERCEPTION	ACTION	 +
SYNTAX	SPACE	
MEANING	DRAWING	 +

Figure 4.1 Action and representational meaning.

reminder of the continued importance of representation as the mode of thinking to avoid alienation from the very frame of reference to which it aims to respond – the context.

When attempting to understand a specific part either of a city or of nature, the constituent parts will present certain psychological connotations that are likely to affect the perception of their organisation.[6] Reading those parts in totality requires perceiving them through multiple frames of reference, which is in effect an innate cerebral process that engages with dialectical relationships – such as fragment–whole, vertical–horizontal and black–white – constituting our basic information system of senses. As a cultural construct, no building is validated without referring to its appropriate frames of reference.[7] Kim Dovey identified this process as action and representation, constituting the main source of human creative endeavour (Figure 4.1).[8] In architecture, drawings have the ability to consider all these references through human perception – of which vision is the primary one – to construct a palpable representation of our built form that is linked to our frames of reference.[9] In visual representation four basic components establish

the fundamentals of an environment: line, shape, colour and texture. Drawings form the transitioning process from conceptual projection to the graphic one, and of our three-dimensional world.

The conception of the drawing as the true delineator of the three-dimensional world – space – dates back to the Italian Renaissance as the process linking ideas to buildings. 'The command of drawing underpins the status of architectural design as intellectual and artistic labour';[10] this command gains its authority from the circumstance as well as history and the intention of the architect who interweaves these into architectural design. Etymologically the term *design* derives from the Italian word *disegno* – the 'drawing' of lines, shapes and forms – and thus for architects *disegno* is more concerned with ideas of architecture than the matter of building. This is for two reasons: first, it is 'seen as the speculative action that encodes architectural thought';[11] and second, 'the architect standing before a building often sees not mass and matter, but form and proportion'.[12] Controlling both form and proportion can never be achieved without the collective quality of drawing.

Therefore, 'the most innovative architectural developments
have risen not from speculation of building, but through
the translation of particular qualities of the drawing to
the building'.[13] Similarly with geometrical compositions,
'without the architect's faith that geometrically defined
lines will engender something else more substantial
yet discernable through the drawing, without faith in
the genetic message inscribed on paper, there is no
architecture'.[14]

Disegno, as craftsmanship, is simply the job of the architect
to illustrate the triadic system of architectural drawing
– plan, section and elevation. Over the second half of
the sixteenth century, the architect-designer legitimised
design as the act of undertaking *disegno*, 'an intellectual,
learned, conceptual, and expert art by adopting the title
"architect"'.[15] This made the architect a master of *disegno*
– not a master of the building craft, acknowledging
Plato's position that matters are inferior to ideas; i.e. the
intellectual labour is superior to the manual one and
thereby essence precedes existence. Patterns conceived by
the architect ensure the influence of the idea over matter.[16]
Conceiving these forms is complemented by certain
meanings and those meanings should emanate in some
way from representation that ensures 'the two domains
of material and the imaginal … are closely and intimately
intertwined',[17] reflecting the architect's comprehension of
the circumstance.

The mediating projection

Through drawing, humanity has found the most appropriate
way of expressing its inherited legacies – thoughts – of
what surrounds us. From the first illustration in prehistory
dating back to the Palaeolithic age 35,000 years ago, to
the computer-generated ones of the present, drawing
still represents and codifies, and dominates our visual
and cultural disciplines. The study of lines as an aesthetic
and psychological representation of human imagination
and perception dates back a long time. The delineation

of beauty, for example, became closely associated with
the profile of distant hills or with the human body,[18] and
psychoanalysts have identified implications of differing
line types in architectural expression. The line is a – if not
the most – 'critical element in the formation of any visual
construction',[19] and has allowed the expression of the
line to be influenced by the profound understanding of
objects and surroundings. The line of beauty reminds us
of those at the chapel of Ronchamp (1955) by Le Corbusier;
its curvilinear plan and form attribute to the lines of the
surrounding hills and the wider setting, whereby the
exterior walls were 'construed as receptors of the four
horizons disclosed at the top of *Bourlement* hill'.[20] Others
have interpreted its organic attributions as representing the
curvaceous lines of the female body.[21]

While verticality in early Gothic architecture emphasised
order and balance – certainly in their interiors – the same
in late Gothic addressed control and force; in contrast, the
Bavarian Baroque was more curvilinear.[22] Two centuries
later, during the first half of the twentieth century,
horizontality was emphasised by both modernism and the
Prairie style as a reaction to the verticality of traditional
architecture. For modernists, it stood as an expression
of the modern culture of industry, of democratic access
to space or as references to the earth's profile. Through
their architectural forms, modern facades impacted
the organisational configuration of plans to read
more rectilinear.[23] In the Prairie style, for instance, the
horizontality of its buildings crystallises the characteristics
of the encompassing terrain, the plains of the American
suburbs. To some extent, this horizontality was reflected in
the organisation of site plans and its considered extension
across and beyond the designated site. This notion was
persistently embodied by Wright in his architecture and
more overtly at Robie House (1906), the lines of which,
both in plan and section, gave the impression that the
house was 'going to glide across the ground to leave only a
vestige of that sea of grass' (Figure 4.2).[24]

076   Enis Aldallal | Site and Composition: Design strategies
Husam AlWaer and | in architecture and urbanism
Soumyen Bandyopadhyay

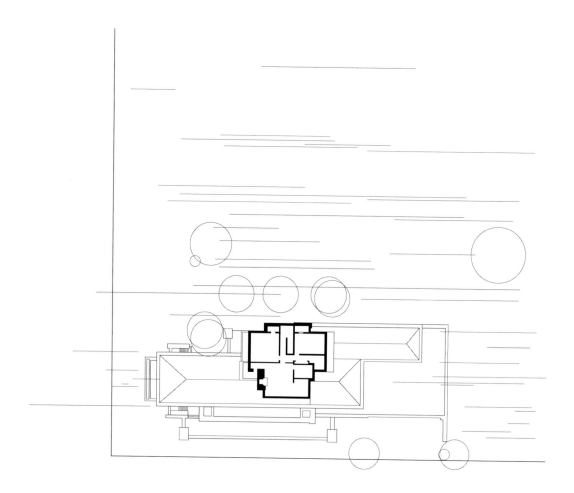

Figure 4.2 Frank L. Wright. Robie House, Chicago, Illinois: third floor plan (after Hoffmann, D., 1984, *Frank Lloyd Wright's Robie House*).

Projection is the process of imprinting that involves
contemplation and representation, both of which play
significant roles in the story of its graphical development.
Since contemplation is actually the imprinted ideas
influenced by vision, they are defined by their implied
references to images. Through the mediating role of
material projection by means of drawing, this bridges the
gap between design 'as an action at a distance'[25] and the
experiences of the moving object or body within buildings.
More significantly, the projection can reveal aspects and
information that cannot automatically be experienced
physically in buildings themselves. In this sense drawing
could be considered as 'the singular vehicle and signifier
that carries the echoes of the architectural ideas and
architectural theories that inhabit it'.[26] Thus, expressing
our ideas through drawings can be achieved by projection,
for 'what connects thinking to imagination; imagination to
drawing; drawing to building; and buildings to our eyes is
projection'.[27] Architectural drawing taken in its entirety of
representational modes constitutes the bridge between
the conceptual and virtual qualities of architecture and its
physical, material manifestation. We dwell in and perceive
architectural intentions through such physicality, as
Pallasmaa succinctly articulates: 'We identify ourselves with
this space; this place; this moment and these dimensions
as they become ingredients of our very existence.'[28] The
discussion in the previous chapter on how the section and
the plan could be valuable devices in dealing with designing
the urban infill will be expanded further, illustrating in
the process both the potential as well as the limitations of
each tool in disclosing the relationships of the site to the
characteristics of its physical setting.

The intrinsic role of section or the tyranny of
the plan

The section has always been an important design tool
in linking architecture to its topographic horizon.[29] With
natural topography, for example, a referential relationship
between architecture and the ground is acknowledged,

at least in construction if not formally, through the action
of excavation, while landscaping (cultivation) is a process
that registers the building onto its definitive topography.
However, some have argued that the 'modern relationship
between construction and topography is best seen in
section (a cutaway drawing), rather than in plan (from
above) or elevation (from outside)'.[30]

Whether manipulated manually or digitally, employed
as the principal generator of design ideas or executed to
complete the set of architectural drawings, the section's
decisive role is undeniable in relating the plan to the
volumetric characteristics of both site and place. At both
the Falling Water and Taliesin West, Wright employs
the section to liberate the plan from its conventional
formal cage of codified organisation but also to address
a sectional configuration that corresponds to the natural
settings. Wright devised the notion of stratification to relate
the encompassing topography with building levels which
theoretically and practically endeavoured to establish a
reciprocal relationship between what was inside and what
was outside.[31] While for Wright and also for Neutra, the bias
towards the sectional configuration emanates directly from
their interest in topography, Stirling's interest in the section
comes from a pictorial standpoint as an experiment to
discover the full potentiality of this tool. He was intrigued
by the sections of nineteenth-century industrial buildings
and found therein a matrix of a new architecture.[32] The
Selwyn College at Cambridge University (1959) is a clear
example of this stance. A few years later, the exercise at
Selwyn College was to prove a good rehearsal for Stirling's
celebrated Engineering Building at the University of
Leicester (1959–63).[33]

The propensity towards sectional configuration can be due
to programmatic interests like those of Bernard Tschumi,
who devised the programme to grant architecture its
unique configuration through section,[34] examples of which
lie in his Sao Paulo Art Museum (2001), Troy Performing Arts
Centre (2001) and New York African Art Museum (2000–2).

078   Enis Aldallal | Site and Composition: Design strategies
Husam AlWaer and | in architecture and urbanism
Soumyen Bandyopadhyay |

Rem Koolhaas' obsession with programme devised through the section 'has helped us to think of architecture vertically … and incorporated the concept of the free section into the architectural culture'.[35]

However, the emphasis on section to generate an entire design is impossible without an appropriate emplacement of its plan, which reveals the limitation of the sectional configuration in isolation. In both Stirling and Tschumi the planimetric configuration featured as an important device of adjustment for the section. In Tschumi's case it was immediate; for example, following a site visit he made, which questioned design thoughts established before the visit through sectional configuration, he contemplated,

The question is whether the building core should be parallel to the site boundary line established by recent history, or perpendicular to the river, along the axis laid by nature. The decision is made to follow nature, as Oscar Niemeyer did in the nearby Memorial da America Latina.[36]

In search of alternative layouts retaining site specificity Tschumi located the auditorium in relation to the street, providing protection to the street's entrance,[37] where planimetric frames of reference appear by necessity. In Stirling's case the shift to plan took much longer than for Tschumi. During the early 1970s, his interest in section started to gravitate towards the plan not only to express

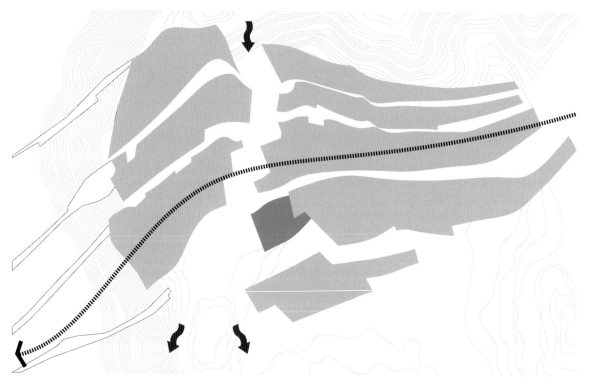

Figure 4.3 Peter Eisenman. The City of Culture of Galicia, Spain: topographic study (after Davidson, C., 2006, Tracing Eisenman).

a compositional bias but as a necessary response to the physical context,[38] as we observe in the Derby Civic Centre (1970) competition entry. Koolhaas' obsession with section and programme is not about visual superposition of planes and layers but a superposition of socio-cultural experiences – it is 'not a visual process but as a form of existence'.[39]

The noted shift in architectural composition from the verticality (section) of the eighteenth and the early nineteenth centuries to the horizontality (plan) of the late nineteenth and twentieth centuries is attributable to changed compositional strategies and cultural understanding of the new industrialised Western world,[40] as well as to the emerging theoretical notions of terrain and topography. Consequently, 'such changes in architecture are most abstractly recorded in spatial manipulations of plan and section'.[41]

Thus the plan appears to have retained significance among many architects as the potential generator of key design ideas and not merely as codified representation. The desire to bring into dialogue the site with its place characteristics has inspired architects to search for varied methods of representation. Planimetric representation came into prominence through Giambattista Nolli's 1748 engraving of the plan of Rome, which in turn drew on the figure–ground representational method initiated by Bufalini (1551). Unlike the perspective, the plan remains true to the key principles of Euclidean geometry;[42] in a non-distorted way it reveals things impossible to actually view otherwise as it shows both the 'projective and unrealized contents'.[43]

In the City of Culture of Galicia project in Spain Peter Eisenman pushes further the boundaries of the figure–ground relationship. Deviating from its Cartesian sense originally employed by Nolli and in more recent times among others by Rowe and Trancik, he claimed that,

> [t]he city of culture develops as powerful new figure–ground urbanism. Rather than see the project as a

series of discrete buildings – the traditional form of figure–ground urbanism – the buildings are literally incised into the ground to form a figure–figure urbanism in which architecture and topography merge to become figures.[44]

Thus Eisenman's novel articulation of the figure–ground relationship involved configuring the ground itself, in this case through Cartesian and simulated topographic impositions, a notion central to the utilisation of the topography of a place, to which we will return later. Planimetric composition does not merely entail geometrical configuration of architectural elements, but establishing means of extracting and employing anew the characteristics of a place.

The belief in the plan as the generative source of architectural invention inspired Le Corbusier and led him to coin the phrase 'architecture is the plan'.[45] Planimetric composition can be the generator not only of geometrical relations among city artefacts but also of spatial settings, which is exemplified by Trachtenberg's investigation into ideal geometrical compositions latent within the medieval urban fabric of Florence. Trachtenberg observed that by inserting the Palazzo Vecchio into the composition of the Piazza della Signoria the piazza was divided into a larger and a smaller piazza related through rotational geometry of the square (Figure 4.4).[46]

Alvaro Siza's sensitivity towards the power of geometry of a place manifests as a sensual, three-dimensional experience in Leça da Palmeira swimming pools (1961–6). The intention was to fuse the pools of the Matosinhos beach next to the old port with its natural topography, resulting in a 'subtle mediation between the coastal road, a rock-strewn site and the open sea'.[47] This mediation was undertaken by austere geometrical projections and transformations which began from the coastal road and the open seaside. The fusion of structure and nature was the ultimate goal of Siza, minimising in the process the amount of blasting of

080   Enis Aldallal | Site and Composition: Design strategies
Husam AlWaer and | in architecture and urbanism
Soumyen Bandyopadhyay |

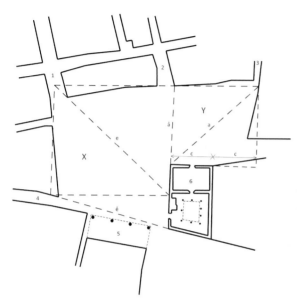

Figure 4.4 Piazza della Signoria, fourteenth century CE, plan (after Temple, N., 2007, *Disclosing Horizons*).

Figure 4.5 Alvaro Siza. Swimming Pools, Leça da Palmeira, Portugal: plan (after Frampton, K. & Siza, A., 2000, *Alvaro Siza: Complete Works*).

the rocks necessary (Figure 4.5). Through the creation of a system of platforms, Siza managed to establish a 'horizontal order' that ensures the amalgamation of the opposites of nature and structure, and of the land and the sea.[48] The floor plans reveal how Siza intentionally fragmented the composition of this building in response to the topographic specifics for enhancing mediation between these opposites. On the side of nature – the sea – the geometry took on a fragmented configuration, while on the counter side, the alignment with the street has followed a more abstract mode. Commenting on Siza's such apparently simple treatment of architectural problems Kenneth Frampton commented:

> The honest and generous modesty with which he responds to each professional opportunity, the conviction which he, himself an excellent story-teller, holds that an architecture is not ugly in its theme, because there are no beautiful or ugly themes in architecture; there is only good or bad treatment of the theme.[49]

Eisenman's *Cities of Artificial Excavation* project, extending over ten years between 1978 and 1988, has showed the creative role of the plan, not only to record site qualities but also its potential to, as he claims, investigate and

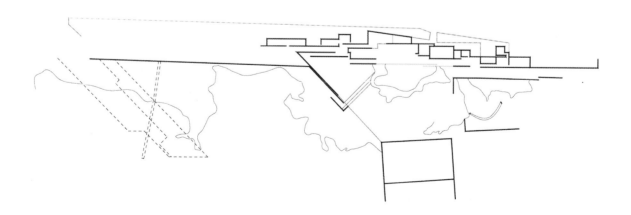

interrogate prevailing architectural discourses, and to instil the poetic[50] aspects of Eisenman's work we aim to illustrate further through his Wexner and Aronoff centres later in this chapter. Unlike Siza and Eisenman, however, Frank Gehry regards both the plan and the section as highly conventional methods of architectural design generation that, for him, should follow the three-dimensional modelling process, emphasising therefore the codificatory qualities of these orthographic projections.

Exclusivism versus inclusivism

In siting practice, to include the physical characteristics of a place means making the best of what an architect finds at her/his disposal. Although this does suggest looking at a site as an independent entity, in effect it has to deal with the site as a fragment interdependent with the existing physical and cultural context. As early as 1752 Antoine Le Paurte echoed this stance through his design for the Hotel de Beauvais, Paris. The floor plans show that the organising lines and resultant spaces of the building were generated by recognising certain alignments with adjacent buildings (Figure 4.6).[51]

The desire to emphasise the independence of a building from its context, derived often from a misunderstood notion of invention, has become associated with the idea of novelty and its representation. In the early part of the twentieth century both architectural independence and invention emerged as reflections of the modernist mentality – its architecture created autonomous narratives and crystallised the claimed invention through the solipsism of its structures, geometries and abstract forms. This denial of surroundings – *exclusivism*, as Cohen suggests[52] – was contrasted by the postmodernists' position of *inclusivism*, which demonstrated at the least their stated willingness to be inflected by context. Exemplified by Venturi's seminal publication, *Complexity and Contradiction in Architecture*, the position held in inclusive architecture is accommodating rather than excluding.[53] Unfortunately, contextual

inflections claimed by the postmodern protagonists became little more than superficial historical analysis of forms and events and their pictorial representations.

The notion of inclusion, either by recognising or by replicating the defining characteristics of the physical settings, is an approach derived from Colin Rowe's planning strategies of *contextualism*.[54] It is different from that of Venturi's in its aversion for certain references to architectural imagery. His inclusivism was to produce a physical, spatial – although literal – continuity of urban form. Yet in Rowe's contextualism Ellis detects a dialectical relationship between postmodern inclusivism and the exclusivism of the modern movement, and suggests this as the key to understanding his approach.[55] His aesthetic tendencies towards the abstract representations of modernism was painted with the admiration of traditional urban fabric. As

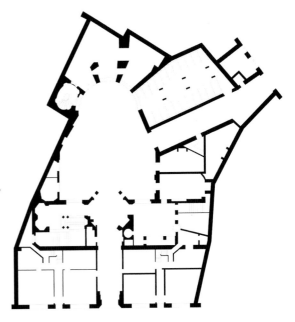

Figure 4.6 Antoine Le Paurte. Hotel de Beauvais, Paris: plans (after Burns & Kahn, eds, 2005 *Site Matters*).

082   Enis Aldallal | Site and Composition: Design strategies
Husam AlWaer and | in architecture and urbanism
Soumyen Bandyopadhyay

Ellis suggests, Rowe's contextualism mitigated two images of the city: '1. the traditional city, with its open space "carved out of solid mass", and 2. Le Corbusier's "city in the park," with its isolated buildings standing free in open space'.[56] Seldom, it seems, is inclusivism solely occupied with the production of pure imagery, and contextualism with physical organisation. The following discussion will therefore address both the inclusivism and the performative abstraction of exclusivism.

Topography as a font of design

One of the most explicit – yet implicit – ingredients of the ground is topography. In the general sense of its employment in architecture, landscape architecture and urbanism, topography is the area between the earth and the sky and 'is the zone rich in living things. In itself, topography sometimes determines a plan. The ingredients of paths, the flow of utilities, the use of areas, the disposition of buildings, and the visual form are all dependent on it.'[57] In this sense, topography seems to possess the explicit characteristics of the ground. Such explicit characteristics notwithstanding, topography is subject to continual evolvement due to the ever-changing nature of its contents through the dimension of time, as Leatherbarrow reminds us.[58] In this sense, topography – both natural and urban – appears to also carry the implicit characteristics of the ground; change is constant in nature, as it is in the city – the latter characterised by the growth and decay of its artefacts.

Going beyond Lynch's understanding of topography as something material, Leatherbarrow argued for its extended phenomenological and perceptual qualities brought forth through the experiences of both familiarity and unexpectedness.[59] Familiar, because it appears tangible and most designers take it for granted as a projected diagram on the survey plan of the site; unexpected, because of its inconsistent qualities that change through the dimension of time. However, to grasp some of its characteristics, topography should necessarily be seen through a wider

lens that transcends the narrow disciplinary boundary of architecture to include landscape architecture and other cognate disciplines. The character of topography is,

> *horizontal*; that movement within it continually confronts contrary conditions and mosaic heterogeneity; that it cannot be equated with land or materials as physical substances; that is not form either, when that is taken to be immaterial volume or profile; that its manner of presenting itself is paradoxical: manifestly latent, or given, not shown; and that its temporality slows it to serve both record of and invitation to human praxis.[60]

Either latent within or immediately apparent, topographical knowledge should be understood and employed just like the more explicit understandings of the site. Through this intellectual and physical engagement, both the figure and the ground can be significantly transformed. For such transformation to take its empirical impact as something material, 'a fairly insistent abstraction is required for acceptance of the space hypothesis … for conditions as concrete as construction materials, modes of production, typical dimensions, and kinds of use need to be neglected to see [the] two' – architecture and landscape architecture – 'as arts of formal composition'.[61] Thus abstraction becomes the process of regenerating sites by articulating their implicit qualities, making those *inclusive*.

Lynch stressed that experienced designers should look at ground in a way that enables them to establish connections with an integrated framework of relations to place.[62] In that sense, 'the vast diversity and unlimited combinational and connective potential of the ground suggests an expansive account of the site', that is, 'an opening to more extensive and varied grounds',[63] that would be involved in the process of making the site. Such ideas were first embodied in the notion of the *completed landscape* of Wright's Falling Water in Pennsylvania and Taliesin East in Wisconsin.[64] Topography reflects the *locus* of a place and, in turn, can be reflected in it;[65] at Taliesin, Wright valued the stratification of stonework to reach the contours of the adjacent hill and read the lines of the adjacent hills as those of the roofs.[66] The concept of *locus* was, as Rossi points out, 'present at all times for the theoretician of the Renaissance'; however, 'by the time of Palladio and later Milizia its treatment took on an increasingly topographical and functional aspect'.[67]

While the natural topography might provide the nearest opportunity for what Dripps has called design free-of-contingency, designing within urban topography is much more heavily contingent on premises that have the ability to direct and shape design ideas. And if Frank Lloyd Wright and Luis Barragan were those who made the natural topography count in their architecture, architects such as Richard Neutra considered the city as an 'evolving topography' in which 'landscape and successive layers of built form intersected over time'.[68] As indicated in the previous chapter, the identifiable topography is not only that which links architecture to nature but also to the city; the reference therefore should not only extend to the natural topography but also to the urban.[69] Robert Morris argued that working with urban sites was restraining to architectural invention compared to rural landscapes, which offered more opportunities and flexibility to the architect to demonstrate his skills.[70] However, the intention here is not to distinguish between two manifestations of cultural landscape; although nature 'influences the concept of landscape today … urban landscape is cultural landscape just as rural landscape is'.[71]

The completing plan: or how topography is both the signified and the signifier

The synthesis that a fragment – a site – should attempt to achieve by means of its instrumental configuration is thus a socio-cultural endeavour. In itself, this strategy is a collaboration of place morphology, the positive-fragmentary qualities of site and the phenomenological characteristics of place topography. Here, place and site are not interchangeable entities; site plays an intrinsic role

in anchoring the sense of place by signifying the common factors between them, that is, through topography.

The discussion that follows illustrates three urban sites in which the architectural object and its surrounding topography are manipulated through the plan. The focus of the first project, Zaha Hadid's 'LF One', is to illustrate the dynamic aspect of topography: the flow and movement of and through the landscape through a pictorial approach. The other two examples drawn from Peter Eisenman's work aim to illustrate the method of signifying the topographical premises through the use of geometry. What Schäfer describes as the necessary focus on the spatial aspects of a place – that is, its enclosures, continuities and extent – 'can also lead to interpretations of its potentials for occupation and use, which are not only or not essentially pictorial but practical'.[72]

Horizontal flow: Zaha Hadid's 'LF One' landscape exhibition

Regardless of the scale of the totality, the notion of flow and continuity are coupled with establishing reciprocal relationships between what is inside and what is outside. 'The consequence of these more concrete continuities between the interiors and their landscape setting', Leatherbarrow contends, 'was that architectural design was discovered to be an art of articulating *topography*'.[73] Zaha Hadid's 'LF One' project for the landscaping exhibition in Weil am Rhein, Germany broadly illustrates this position, which straddles the boundaries between architecture and urbanism. Allowing flow, the architect has invited the paths of the embracing urban landscape into the site configuration to overlap with spaces and activities of the architectural objects. Movement through landscape 'follows paths others have taken. This is especially true for landscapes that have been designed; in contrast to those that exist by nature, for designed sites normally set out lines of movement that visitors are expected to follow.'[74] To facilitate movement *through* landscape, 'LF One' is argued to

084   Enis Aldallal | Site and Composition: Design strategies
Husam AlWaer and | in architecture and urbanism
Soumyen Bandyopadhyay |

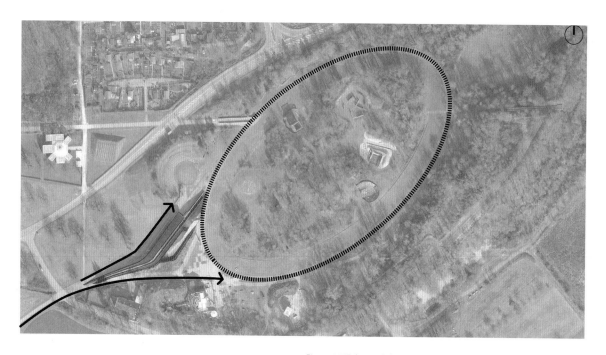

Figure 4.7 Zaha Hadid. LF-One Exhibition Landscape, Weil am Rhein, Germany: the dynamic plan.

have been designed as 'part of a sequence of projects that try to elicit new fluid spatialities from the study of natural landscape formations such as river deltas, mountain ranges, forests, deserts, canyons, ice-flow, and so on'.[75]

The site is surrounded by grassy mounds, waving at certain corners and disappearing at others. Pathways tangentially meet a pre-existing elliptical route that extends in a great ring through the wider landscape of the site (Figure 4.7). Hadid, however, considers that landscape features take precedence over a geometry that lies latent in the milieu of site, alluding to the need for foregrounding anthropo-cultural parameters within the pictorial depiction. In other words, the project is 'conceived in terms of landscape features rather than in terms of geometry'.[76] The 'LF One' is 'not substantial on its own terms, nor self-sufficient', but partially 'contingent, dependent or adjective to its milieu'.[77]

The existing landscape, as the architect suggests,

is taken as a starting point for the project's development. Contours of building-object emerge steadily, step by step, in relation to the surroundings, while internally the building itself becomes a landform, with a rich repertoire of earth-related features such as mounts, ramps, excavation, erosions, abrasions, tiered land, eruptions. Projects of such nature might generate vigorous energetic, twist-and-turn buildings, or they might be more subdued and clamming acting from the depth of the earth and liquefying like a tidal wave or lava flow.[78]

The building thus acts as a quasi-natural entity that grows out of the ground, overlapping with the paths, which in turn brings the building back to the ground. 'Physically

and formally embedded into the large and topographically
rich garden space', the building affirms its topographical
rootedness as part of its wider place experience.[79]

The existing landscape is abstracted by deciphering
the site's geometry in which contours are extended
into the building, developing an *alternative* ground
within, intertwined with occupancy and use. Given its
derivation from and deep engagement with the physical
characteristics of the surrounding place, the boundary
between the site and its surroundings becomes less
defined. Such ambiguity, however, should not be confused
with the dissolution of the 'site' altogether through
excessive flow.[80] While the alternative landscape inside
overlaid with specific programmatic concern distinguishes
it from the outside, the fusing of the paths of the site and
those of the landscape manifests mutual interdependency,
ensuring that the 'structure does not sit in the landscape as
an isolated object, but emerges from the fluid geometry of
the surrounding network of paths'.[81]

Though largely inspired by a figurative approach, the
intention of 'LF One' in portraying and integrating with
the surrounding landscape turns the site into an ambient
landscape, which 'enters into, continues through, emanates
from, and enlivens it'.[82] Such intertwining of architecture
and landscape architecture did not lead to the defeat
of either; instead, as Hadid claimed, 'landscape spaces
remain flexible and open … whereas architecture generally
channels, segments and closes, landscape opens, offers and
suggests. This does not mean that we abandon architecture
and surrender to brute nature.'[83]

Here, nature becomes the programme for architecture. At
'LF One' horizontal movement manifests itself in two ways;
first, in the dynamic design of the building – an object
animating its wider space – the landscape; and second,
resulting from the first, the somatic movement through
the building which reads as a landscape feature, 'wherein
the viewing body negotiates between landscape-as-

representation and landscape-as-experience'.[84] Hence,
rooting the building within its landscape makes its 'somatic
program engage one's syncopated movement into and
through the … complex',[85] that intertwine both kinds of
movement. In that sense, topography has granted the
'figure' (the building) a non-conventional relationship
with the 'ground', distinct from the *Cartesian* relationship
discussed earlier.

Emergent fragment: Peter Eisenman's Wexner Centre

Some critics have called it a 'crazy building'.[86] Eisenman's
Wexner Centre for the Visual Arts in Columbus, Ohio (1989)
has acquired this epithet due to its strangely juxtaposed
architectural elements, very much like a collagist working
(Figure 4.8). However, it is the unique, radical engagement
with site that this discussion aims to examine; as Moneo
puts it, 'it is difficult to understand the Ohio State Centre
for the Visual Arts without talking about the site'.[87]
This discussion aims to illustrate how architecture, as a
fragment of a wider framework, could act as the 'keystone'
completing topographic relationships within a locale. The
urban topographical premises of this site are: the pre-
existing buildings – Mershon Auditorium and the Weigel
Hall – 'the Oval' of Ohio State University Campus and the
surrounding framework of routes, the High Street and the
15th and 17th avenues. All these entities, as well as the
Armory – a building to the west of the site recorded and
demolished in 1959 – form the premises of Eisenman's
design for the Wexner Centre.

Given Eisenman's obsession with process and method, it
is important that each entity is discussed independently.
In terms of composition, the site has been understood as
a connective entity between the city and the campus. For
Eisenman, 'architecture is part of culture – a cultural artefact
like a piece of literature, a painting, a piece of music …
Architecture does something the other arts do not do. It
brings together the physical experience of moving.'[88] The

086   Enis Aldallal | Site and Composition: Design strategies
       Husam AlWaer and | in architecture and urbanism
    Soumyen Bandyopadhyay |

Figure 4.8 Peter Eisenman. The Wexner Centre for the Visual Arts, Ohio State University, Columbus, Ohio: view looking north.

Wexner Centre should not only be perceived in the light of the immediately surrounding context, it is important that it be read in the light of its socio-cultural networks extending through the city. Eisenman has conceded that his de-contextualised projects, House I to Xia, revealed for him that 'architecture needs to "include" outside parameters in order to be produced, and that only in the frame of its external circumstance does it acquire meaning'.[89]

The pre-existing buildings

Flanking the Wexner on the east, built in 1957 and operated by the Wexner Centre since 1989, the Mershon Auditorium is a premier venue for the performing arts, lectures and multimedia presentations.[90] The Weigel Hall, which flanks the Wexner on the west is, on the other hand, a performance venue that belongs to the Ohio State University School of Music. Eisenman's proposal for the Wexner Centre re-collected both buildings under its umbrella, besides adding exhibition galleries, a library, bookshop, additional performance hall, café, video theatre, offices, and a multi-purpose auditorium to occupy 130,000 square feet in total. The scheme of the Centre embraced these two pre-existing buildings, which, 'stretched and enveloped, took on a new significance';[91] its somewhat self-effacing profile pushes out beyond these encompassing structures.[92] The two flanking buildings have inflected the formal language of the Wexner Centre. The western side of the gallery is aligned with the Weigel, giving rise to subtle reconfigurations of the interiors of the galleries. It also resulted in the duct-like objects running on the roof ending up with a sharply tapered, almost nautical object of limited functionality that flows over the scaffold (Figure 4.9).[93] On the east side the impact is reversed as Eisenman 'shaves a corner off' the Mershon; however, 'the wound is camouflaged: a new wall

constructed along the line of the shear seamlessly blends with old, obliterating any evidence of the transformation'.[94]

This apparently simple impact requires further consideration to illustrate Eisenman's distinctive take on site and context – an approach that suggests a re-evaluation of the role of instrumental means of enriching planimetric composition, expanding manyfold the potential content a site and its context could offer. The new intervention

Figure 4.9 The Wexner Centre: the boat-like object resulting from alignment with the Weigel Hall.

does not simply fit within the space available between two buildings, acting in the limited capacity of an urban infill. It physically transmits a received impact from one on to the other, distorting and reshaping, and thereby more profoundly connecting, two previously unconnected buildings – which are now presented as site fragments. Such linkages extend beyond those originally suggested and lay latent within the site; here Eisenman's building itself acts as a catalytic fragment – an embryonic graft – that serves as an instigator for establishing new relationships. For Eisenman the *graft* is essential to make incursions into the solipsistic interiority of the project and its context. In the graft we observe a 'motivation for action that begins a process which relies on its internal structures. The graft begins with the heterogeneously unstable, and through a process of artificial conjunction extracts a motivation upon which the modification can take place.'[95] The insertion of his earlier House 11a into the design for Cannaregio West in Venice is one of the earliest of such initiatives, along with the continuation of the grid resulting from Le Corbusier's earlier Venice Hospital project.[96] We will discuss shortly the impact of the grid that dominates at Wexner.

These impositions or graftings on a site and their processual extensions, manipulations and ramifications, dealt with in their entirety in the abstract, suspended all familiar historical and topographical analogy – or what Jameson called textually reliant 'allegorical patterns' present within humanist architecture[97] – and emphasised instead graphical means internal to architecture. Through this graphical exercise, Eisenman's *artificial excavation* projects thus developed a new form of a-textual architectural fiction reliant on geometric manipulation through what he called 'superpositions', resulting in an entirely artificial 'hypercondition'.[98] These apparently 'monologic' manipulations of applied geometries, emancipated from the actual site settings, have been criticised for confusing what is actually meant by the 'dialogic' nature of sites. However, such accusations may not be entirely valid; the meta-fictional horizons generated by Wexner and other

projects of this phase are ultimately reliant on particular conditions found in and around the sites, albeit catalysed by imposition of extraneous objects. The ground, in itself, is treated as an object of investigation and no longer as a passive frame.[99] His self-confessed anxiety while seeking to legitimise projects has reintroduced fragments and traces of history, as well as fiction. This is evident in his South Friedrichstadt project in Berlin, where the eighteenth-century wall running through the site was considered. In fact, dialogical relationships open up on many fronts; a series of 'betweenness' are evoked 'as a kind of third party to his various dualisms'.[100]

Landscape, the Oval and the promenade

The landscaping of the forecourts played an important role in rendering material the abstract investigations proposed in the processual build-up to the building's design. Two landscapes were contemplated and implied at the Wexner's forecourts by the landscape architect Laurie Olin to signify the topographic characteristics of both the immediate site and the wider place. First, on the north-eastern side, is the expansive American 'natural' landscape – the Prairie terrains – which appears at the edges of the Wexner and all around (Figure 4.10).[101] Through this Olin implied linkages with elements that constituted for the Wexner a

Figure 4.10 The Wexner Centre: north-eastern forecourt, view looking west.

Figure 4.11 The Wexner Centre: south-eastern forecourt, view looking west.

'more distant horizon'.[102] Second, the American 'urban' landscape embodied by the Jeffersonian grid charting the American north-west (beginning with the eastern part of Ohio state in the 1780s) and impacting on the city designs that followed;[103] this appears on the south-eastern part of the site and intertwines with the north-eastern one (Figure 4.11). At differing scales, the geometry of the building's front court and the plantings are illustrative, as Leatherbarrow points out, of 'contextuality by conformity to preexisting conditions were it not for the fact that each also diverged from what was given and radically reformed the premises that were prearranged'.[104]

Here, again, another grafting appears to be at play in Olin's landscape – an insertion of thickness and tactility within the abstract orthogonality of Eisenman's site organisation. The sudden, unexpected rise of the front retaining wall from knee to waist height instigates a sequence of deviations, making the retaining wall rise in some places to a full human height, questioning the relationship between substrate and surface, as well as the regional and urban landscape paradigms indicated above. What Olin describes as 'walking into the earth, but not' in effect is a strategy that links the planimetric grid linkages developed between buildings, and within the revised campus plan, with the vertical grid of the building's facade – an experiential intervention reconciling the

planimetric with the vertical/sectional. The linear nature of the geometry – Eisenmanian, Jeffersonian and the Prairie – is thus made palpable through the extended experience of the passage leading to the entrance.[105] This further highlights the collective – or collaborative – nature of the overall 'patchwork' intervention in which the materiality of Olin's landscape textualises the a-textual fiction begun by Eisenman's geometries.

The Oval, on the other hand, as a remarkable landscape feature of the campus, has been a controversial point both in designing and evaluating the project. Before the advent of the Wexner, the Oval gained its significance through its axis, which extended into the campus street matrix. Following the introduction of the Wexner, the Oval took on a different significance – as a key landscape feature that now oriented the buildings of the campus. The axis was substituted by the extension of the 15th Avenue, which now deviated by 12.25 degrees from it, 'creating a shift that allows a distinction between the campus and the surrounding neighbourhoods'.[106] In conjunction with the landscape of the forecourts, this move extended the *promenade architecturale* through a piece of American urban landscape, combining the experience of a 'romantic view of the past and an anticipation of the future' (Figure 4.12).[107] Together, they form a new 'betweenness', unfolding an engagement with two distinct sets of dualisms: on the one hand, the city grid and the campus plan, and on the other, the nineteenth- and twentieth-century nature of the campus itself represented through two distinctive – but nevertheless determining – geometries: the elliptical and the orthogonal.

The geometry and the defining grid

Running perpendicular to the 15th Avenue and strongly representative of the American urban landscape, the north–south axis of the site penetrated and bisected it. Eisenman's approach in completing the topographical relationships on this site is geometrical, and although some of his devices appear instrumental, the results are

090   Enis Aldallal | Site and Composition: Design strategies
Husam AlWaer and | in architecture and urbanism
Soumyen Bandyopadhyay |

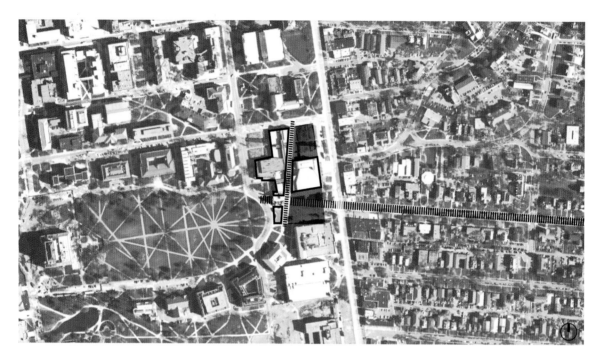

Figure 4.12 The Wexner Centre: the relationship between the Oval and the city.

non-formal, and even phenomenological.[108] The geometry embodied by the grid system emerges as 'structural elements, as windows, as dark grey stripes skidding across light grey carpet, as cuts in walls or indentations in ceilings, as a Bosque'.[109] Some critics have argued that the grid is entirely decorative, and Eisenman would probably agree about the old-fashioned, ornamental anti-functionality of his grid. Being neither entirely instrumental nor forming a structural system (although both of them are virtually synonymous in practice),[110] the grid 'stands as the merciless demonstration … of conflict in the mapping of the real. … The grid seems to hover between the infinite and the bounded, ambiguous and refusing all narratives of a single point of origin.'[111] The grid at the Wexner implies two essential readings: first, it is an obvious metaphor for the Jeffersonian mapping

technique of the American urban landscape; and second, it works as a fragment of a wider abstracted framework that aims to connect, complete and perform a higher system of synthesis. Yet, in most American cities the grid is an instrument of synthesis of 'disparate materials … partial forms, linguistic phenomena, social and psychological raw material, semi-autonomous ideological fantasies, local period concepts, scientific spare parts, and random topical themes'.[112] The fragments are never fused into a singular, resolved synthesis, however; instead, the coexistence of disparate entities only nominally held together by the grid, as Jameson suggests, points towards an essentially unresolvable set of contradictions[113] – between past and present, between histories, between the mindset of the individual author/architect and the factual and material conditions of the project and site, and so on.

*The fragmented palimpsest and the articulated
excavation*

The Wexner 'can be described as non-building – an
archaeological earthwork whose essential elements are
scaffolding and landscaping' – the key components we
have just discussed.[114] Besides the scaffolding, the brick
towers at the centre are among the most controversial
elements because of their incompleteness (Figure 4.13).
Architecture has always played an important role in
reconciling the present and the past. The significance of
the towers lies in their challenging role in the recollection

of the particularities of place history and their preparation
for the demands of the future. Thus, 'the concern for the
particularities of place is linked to the manner in which place
is the site for dwelling, the locus for collective memory, and
the materialization of a history'.[115]

As Leatherbarrow argues, 'the presence of the past in the
present can never be full, however, for then the past as
past would cease to exist'. We commonly term this reduced
presence as the experience that 'encounters traces of events
that occurred before. A trace such as this is fragmentary,
a remnant or vestige'.[116] The original Armory of Ohio State

Figure 4.13 The Wexner Centre: brick presence.

092   Enis Aldallal | Site and Composition: Design strategies
Husam AlWaer and | in architecture and urbanism
Soumyen Bandyopadhyay |

Figure 4.14 The Wexner Centre: a tower trace; half-sunk, half-exposed presence within the site's topography.

University dated back to the nineteenth century and was demolished in 1959. Resurrecting this latent topographical premise thus necessitated artificial extraction employing texts and drawings to access its historical stratigraphy. For Eisenman those brick towers 'mark the absence of their former presence: their presence is nothing but an absence'.[117] Monumentality was one of the attributes Eisenman read in the brick towers which he wanted to reintroduce: '[a]t first glance, indeed, the building seems to aspire to and achieve a monumentality of impeccable properties'.[118] In the partial resurrection of the tower another characteristic of the graft is put forward; the graft both gestures towards a form of reconciliation between past and present, yet it deconstructs through centrifugal dissociation the very ingredients constituting that relationship – form, materiality, collective and personal memories, historical content. Thus, for Vidler, what remains after the scattering is the abstracted essence of architectural composition that underlies 'all the traditional arts, which signalled authority, whether exhibited in physiognomy, costume, music or painting'.[119] Freeing the form from its previous stylistic shackles underscores the recessive nature of the historical trace.

The physical engagement between the new and the pre-existing, the emergent figure and its latent ground, the site

geometry and the geometry of its context, attempted to not only produce a tangible experience but also a deeper socio-cultural one, calling into question the claim of some that the Wexner Centre was a purely formal exercise with a mere iconographic depiction of a past. Here, Eisenman's objective was to depict all the topographical premises – real and fictional – discovered in the process of producing the architecture. The architecture, rooted both in the explicit, as well as the implicit, embedded and potential premises of the site,[120] also engaged in the articulation of its past by reconstructing the Armory's fragmentary traces (Figure 4.14). It addresses the topography's capacity to 'receive and record more legible articulations because it serves as receptacle'.[121]

Mediation: Peter Eisenman's Aronoff Centre for the Arts

If '[t]he design of the Wexner centre dwells on the ghost of a bygone tower and the skeletal traces of a historic path', the Aronoff Centre for Arts hinges on 'total dematerialization and further intensification of the aesthetic of abstraction' (Figure 4.15).[122] The mission for Eisenman was to add the Aronoff Centre to the College of Design, Architecture, Art and Planning (DAAP) to house recognised programmatic elements of exhibition, library, theatre, studio and office spaces of 13,400 m². An architectural response to place specificity in the 1970s, largely supported by the postmodernists of that period such as Robert Venturi, Aldo Rossi and Michael Graves, advocated the appropriation and re-articulation of the icons and motifs found in and around the site. For Eisenman, however, in the *artificial excavation* projects which culminated in the only fully realised building in the series, the Wexner Centre, this articulation achieved a distinctive methodological dimension characterised by the use of abstraction in the identification, fictionalisation and appropriation of the pre-existing topography. Once again at the Aronoff, where the definitive topography is both natural and urban, 'the curves of the land and chevron forms of the existing building set up a dynamic relationship to organize

Figure 4.15 Peter Eisenman. The Aronoff Centre for the Arts, University of Cincinnati, Cincinnati, Ohio.

the space between the two'.[123] The Aronoff Centre extended Eisenman's interest in the artificial excavation process of site, to extend and establish the site's true domain beyond its physical limits, and connect with a widely extended web of ideas.[124]

The first step in designing the Aronoff Centre was to identify the delineation of the pre-existing buildings of the DAAP. In plan, its eight-foot-wide corridor, often described as the chevron,[125] had its dimensions extended across the site and pre-existing buildings. This ligature was identified as a departure point for establishing the architectural language

of mediation with the urban fabric through different angular shifts to form multiple traces of the original body of the DAAP (Figure 4.16). The result is the composite trace, which when coupled with the plan of the existing buildings, created a hallucinating blur between the original and the trace.[126] Projecting the original and the trace through superimposition created a third form that effectively *intertwined* the forms.[127] It formed 'one of the devices that connect[ed] the existing buildings with new construction while also connecting the new construction to the site and surrounding streets'.[128]

094   Enis Aldallal │ Site and Composition: Design strategies
Husam AlWaer and │ in architecture and urbanism
Soumyen Bandyopadhyay │

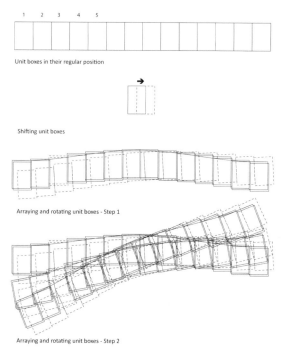

Unit boxes in their regular position

Shifting unit boxes

Arraying and rotating unit boxes - Step 1

Arraying and rotating unit boxes - Step 2

Figure 4.16 The Aronoff Centre: compositional process of the curve(s) (after Davidson, C., ed., *Eleven Authors in Search of a Building*).

interlocking patterns – of boxes – giving rise to the curved line. In fact, the undulating nature of the surrounding mountains could be seen to be embodied in the resultant curve of the Aronoff, giving a shape of a reptilian body that presses itself against the sloping contours of the site.[131] The new addition, as Fredwest concludes, appears to respond better to the form of the surrounding landscape, more than the existing building.[132]

To blur the boundaries between the various fragments, the resulting curve was juxtaposed with the chevron traces. These traces found literal reverberations in both the torqued boxes of the new building but also in the landscape. The blurring gave birth to an interstitial spatial condition, a 'communicative space' (see Chapter 3), which emerged through the process of design.[133] The building resulting from these seemingly inextricably connected fragments read as a whole,[134] resulting in a true space of mediation between the DAAP and the Aronoff to overlap not only their topographies but also their respective activities (Figure 4.17).

Conclusion: emergent composition

Inspired by the undulating, natural topography that surrounded the site, the new building line emerged through proportional construction that used geometry of overlaps and tilts to generate a curvilinear configuration that corresponded to the phase of the chevron.[129] The complex and abstract derivation of the curve resulted in a close correspondence – an approximation, not imitation – that distinguished Eisenman's approach from those of the postmodernists. If we accept that imitation seeks to affirm exactly what exists which at times tolerates modification,[130] the Aronoff is neither imitation nor modification; it is mediation. From the rectilinear profile of the existing to the curvilinear configuration of the new, the process of repeating the unit box identifies a recursive system of

Through time and space, the growth of cities as a whole acquired its significance from the juxtaposed urban infill projects influenced by both zoning and building codes and by the aesthetic awareness of designers. In both codes the control of the building bulk is influenced more by the planimetric configuration (i.e. setbacks, FAR, open space ratio, and so on) than by its section (i.e. bulk plane restriction). The synthesis phase of site – represented by projection – is a response to any emergent issue during the analysis phase – represented by search – to accommodate the many overlapping factors including the codes.

The normative human reaction to an emergent issue is representative in nature; designers and artists react to the perception of a place through representations that usually take the form of texts or drawings, and sometimes both. Place is the generic term for the world that encompasses

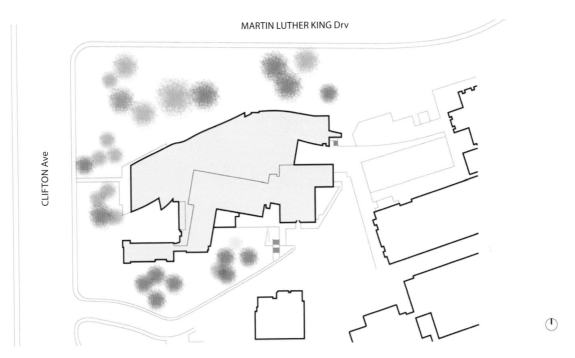

MARTIN LUTHER KING Drv

CLIFTON Ave

Figure 4.17 The Aronoff Centre: site composition showing relationship with the DAAP (after Davidson, C., ed., *Eleven Authors in Search of a Building*).

both our built forms and actions. The architect's interpretation of a place must be accompanied by two substantial sorts of projections: the intellectual projection manifested by contemplation, followed by the second stage of physical projection, manifested by drawing. This process of architectural representation is mutually inseparable, as it is the convergence of three substantial relationships: site–mind, mind–drawing and, finally, drawing–site. The first and the last stages concern our bodily experience with place, chronologically (i.e. before and after its execution). The middle stage is what Robin Evans has called the *'projective cast'* between them, through which the transformation of contemplation takes place through graphical representation. These three stages resemble in sequence the relationship of site and place mentioned earlier, that is,

place–site–place, to be revisited in Chapters 5 and 6, in terms of spatial experience and materiality, respectively.

The significance of this sequence lies in representing graphically the ideas developed between place, our intellect, paper and place again, as the location of material manifestation (building). This approach to siting practice looks at 'place' through a morphological lens devised by the topography of that place, the instrumental basis of which has been elaborated in this chapter in conjunction with the idea of projection. Projection transcends its literal meaning to a much deeper one: it includes – not rejects – the physical characteristics of a place. Because topography is one of the most significant characteristics of ground, and since the urban topography is our main focus, this

096   Enis Aldallal | Site and Composition: Design strategies
Husam AlWaer and | in architecture and urbanism
Soumyen Bandyopadhyay |

chapter has argued that bringing those characteristics into sectional configuration has its limitations unless aided by planimetric study. This is due to the difficulty the sectional approach is confronted with when manipulating the situation and placement within and in relation to a context's topographic horizon. Therefore, many designers have developed their ideas from the plan in their attempt to relate their designs to the surrounding settings. Hence, the defining contextuality of this book is neither to continue with nor to imitate – tectonically or typologically – the existing patterns and images. The completion sought and argued in this chapter is one that is devised by the positive fragmentary qualities of the site, through which both the new and the pre-existing can achieve theoretical transformation that establishes a pattern with the urban fabric, yet preserves their identities.

Addressing a design concept in accordance with existing conditions does not mean

> that the patterns and situations by which topographies are known need to manifest themselves in the same materials (as if isohylic), nor be spatially continuous (isotropic), nor given the same shape and profile (isomorphic); instead, they have to accommodate similar performance, each serving as a receptacle and 'signing' in its own way.[135]

Peter Eisenman's approach in the 1980s – articulated through the *artificial excavation* projects and perhaps best exemplified in the Wexner Centre, the only fully realised building in the series – identified a way forward that relied on a-textual fictive site formations resulting from manipulations and abstractions of site geometry reliant on instrumental moves. In this, the role of the 'foreign' introduction – grafting – as an experiential moment is crucial; at Wexner, as we realise, it congeals but also dissociates – laying bare the site's historical essence (composition) through a process of deconstruction. The grafting of the experiential through Olin's forecourt design

reconciles the abstract exploration of the horizontal with the equally abstract treatment of the vertical.

Notes

1 Leatherbarrow, D., *The Roots of Architectural Invention*, Cambridge: Cambridge University Press, 1993, p. 18.

2 For a detailed discussion by Dalibor Vesely on the nature of the fragment and its potential, see Vesely, D., *Architecture in the Age of Divided Representation: The Question of Creativity in the Shadow of Production*, Cambridge, MA: MIT Press, 2004, pp. 317–354.

3 Spens, M., 'Site/Non-Site: Extending the Parameters in Contemporary Landscape', *Journal of Architectural Design* 77(2), 2007, p. 7.

4 Herbert, D., 'Graphic Process in Architectural Study Drawings', *Journal of Architectural Education* 46(1), 1992, p. 28.

5 Evans, R., *The Projective Cast*, Cambridge, MA: MIT Press, 1995, p. 282.

6 Smith, P., *The Syntax of Cities*, London: Hutchinson, 1977, p. 69.

7 Connah, R., *Writing Architecture: Fantômas, Fragments, Fictions – An Architectural Journey Through the Twentieth Century*, Cambridge, MA: MIT Press, 1989, p. 235.

8 Dovey, K., *Framing Places: Mediating Power in Built Form*, New York: Routledge, 1999, p. 50.

9 Hill, J., 'Building the Drawing', *Architectural Design* (Special issue: *Design Through Making*) 75(4), 2005, p. 17.

10 Ibid.

11 Schneider, P., 'Disegno: On Drawing Out the Archi-texts', *Journal of Architectural Education* 61(1), 2007, p. 20.

12 Hill, op. cit., p. 15.

13 Ibid., p. 17.

14 Evans, op. cit., p. xxvi.

15 Schneider, op. cit., p. 19.

16 Tschumi, B., *Architecture and Disjunction*, Cambridge, MA: MIT Press, 1996, p. 38.

17 Franck, K. & Lepori, R., *Architecture from the Inside Out*, London: Wiley Academy, 2007, p. 157.

18 Smith, *The Syntax of Cities*, p. 69.

19 Ching, F., *Architecture: Form, Space, & Order*, New York: John Wiley, 1996, p. 8.

20 Herbert, op. cit., p. 28.

21 See, for example, Evans, op. cit., p. 284.

22 Smith, *The Syntax of Cities*, p. 73.

23 Schumacher, T., 'Horizontality: The Modernist Line', *Journal of Architectural Education* 59(1), 2005, p. 17.

24 Hoffmann, D., *Frank Lloyd Wright's Robie House: The Illustrated Story of an Architectural Masterpiece*, New York: Dover Publications, 1984, p. 19.

25 Evans, op. cit., p. 363.

26 Schneider, op. cit., pp. 19–20.

27 Evans, op. cit., p. xxxi.

28 Pallasmaa, J., 'An Architecture of the Seven Senses', in Holl, S., Pallasmaa, J. & Gómez, A., *Questions of Perception: Phenomenology of Architecture*, Tokyo: A+U Publishing; San Francisco: William Stout Publishers, 1994 (2007 reprint), p. 29.

29 See Leatherbarrow, D., *Uncommon Ground*, Cambridge, MA: MIT Press, 2002, p. 170.

30 Muschamp, H., 'Art/Architecture: How Modern Design Remains Faithful to its Context', *New York Times*, 6 August 2000: http://query.nytimes.com/gst/ullhtml?res=9B0DE4DD113DF935A3575BC0A9669C8B63&sec=&spon=&pagewanted=all, accessed 30 March 2015.

31 Leatherbarrow, *Uncommon Ground*, p. 43.

32 Moneo, R., *Theoretical Anxiety and Design Strategies in the Work of Eight Contemporary Architects*, Cambridge, MA: MIT Press, 2004, p. 9.

33 Ibid., p. 24.

34 Tschumi, B., *Event City 3*, Cambridge, MA: MIT Press, 2004, pp. 239–389.

35 Moneo, op. cit., p. 318.

36 Tschumi, *Event City 3*, p. 249.

37 Ibid., p. 261.

38 Moneo, op. cit., p. 28.

39 Ibid., p. 317.

098 Enis Aldallal | Site and Composition: Design strategies
Husam AlWaer and | in architecture and urbanism
Soumyen Bandyopadhyay |

40 Eisenman, P., 'Aspects of Modernism: Maison Dom-ino and the Self-Referential Sign', in Hays, M. (ed.), *Oppositions Reader: Selected Readings from a Journal for Ideas and Criticism in Architecture 1973–1984*, New York: Princeton Architectural Press, 1998, p. 189.

41 Ibid.

42 Robbins, E., *Why Architects Draw*, Cambridge, MA: MIT Press, 1994, p. 133.

43 Leatherbarrow, *Roots of Architectural Invention*, p. 67.

44 Lynn, G., 'The City of Culture of Galicia', in Davidson, C. (ed.), *Tracing Eisenman*, London: Thames & Hudson, 2006, p. 308.

45 Ibid., p. 9.

46 Temple, N., *Disclosing Horizons: Architecture, Perspective and Redemptive Space*, London and New York: Routledge, 2007, pp. 113–114.

47 Frampton, K., *Alvaro Siza: Complete Works*, London: Phaidon, 2000, p. 16.

48 Moneo, op. cit., p. 213.

49 Frampton, op. cit., p. 7.

50 Bédard, J.-F., 'Introduction', in Bédard, J.-F. (ed.), *Cities of Artificial Excavation: The Work of Peter Eisenman, 1978–1988*, Montreal and New York: Canadian Centre for Architecture & Rizzoli International, 1994, p. 13–16.

51 Dripps, R., 'Groundwork', in Burns, C., & Kahn, A. (eds), *Site Matters: Design Concepts, Histories and Strategies*, New York and Abingdon: Routledge, 2005, p. 76.

52 Cohen, S., 'Physical Context/Cultural Context: Including it All', in Hays, M. (ed.), *Oppositions Reader: Selected Readings from a Journal for Ideas and Criticism in Architecture 1973–1984*, New York: Princeton Architectural Press, 1998, p. 66.

53 Ibid.

54 Ibid., p. 67.

55 Ellis, W., 'Type and Context in Urbanism: Colin Rowe's Contextualism', in Hays, M. (ed.), *Oppositions Reader: Selected Readings from a Journal for Ideas and Criticism in Architecture 1973–1984*, New York: Princeton Architectural Press, 1998, p. 228.

56 Ibid.

57 Lynch, K., *Site Planning*, Cambridge, MA: MIT Press, p. 39.

58 Leatherbarrow, *Uncommon Ground*, p. 176.

59 Leatherbarrow, 'Topographical Premises', *Journal of Architectural Education* 57(3), 2004, p. 70.

60 Ibid.

61 Leatherbarrow, D., *Topographical Stories: Studies in Landscape and Architecture*, Pennsylvania: University of Pennsylvania Press, 2004, p. 4.

62 Lynch, op. cit., p. 41.

63 Dripps, op. cit., p. 71.

64 Smith, P., *Architecture and the Principle of Harmony*, London: RIBA, 1987, p. 8.

65 Rossi explains: 'Locus: is the relationship of a certain specific location to the buildings that are in it'. See, Rossi, A., *The Architecture of the City*, Cambridge, MA: MIT Press, 1982, p. 103.

66 Leatherbarrow, *Uncommon Ground*, pp. 186–187.

67 Rossi, op. cit., p. 103.

68 Muschamp, op. cit.

69 Leatherbarrow, *Uncommon Ground*, p. 211.

70 Leatherbarrow, *Topographical Stories*, p. 177.

71 Schäfer, R., 'Landscape', in Wingårdh , G. & Wærn, R. (eds), *Crucial Words: Conditions for Contemporary Architecture*, Berlin: Birkhauser, 2008, p. 112.

72 Leatherbarrow, *Topographical Stories*, p. 10.

73 Leatherbarrow, *Uncommon Ground*, p. 176.

74 Leatherbarrow, *Topographical Stories*, p. 200.

75 El Croquis/Hadid, Z., 'Zaha Hadid (1983–2004)', *El Croquis* 53/73 (I)/103, Madrid: El Croquis, 2004, p. 290.

76 www.archidose.org/oct,99, accessed 22 June 2007.

77 Leatherbarrow, *Topographical Stories*, p. 20.

78 Hadid, Z., 'Explosions; Compressions; Swarms, Aggressions, Pixelations; Carved Spaces, Excavations', in Jencks, C. & Kropf, K. (eds), *Theories and Manifestoes of Contemporary Architecture*, London: Wiley Academy, 2006, p. 365.

79 El Croquis/Hadid, Z., op. cit., p. 290.

80 Leatherbarrow points out that, 'The privileging of flowing space

also eliminates the possibility of locating distinct sites, for when continued passage is always possible boundaries can never be fixed, and a site without edges is not a site at all'. Leatherbarrow, *Uncommon Ground*, p. 180.

81 www.pritzkerprize.com/2004/pdf/LFOne.pdf, accessed 6 February 2008, p. 3.

82 Leatherbarrow, *Topographical Stories*, p. 21.

83 El Croquis/Hadid, Z., op. cit., p. 304.

84 Dodds, G., 'Desiring Landscapes/Landscapes of Desire: Scopic and Somatic in the Brion Sanctuary', in Dodds, G. & Tavernor, R. (eds), *Body and Building*, Cambridge, MA: MIT Press, 2002, p. 240.

85 Ibid.

86 Andersen, K., 'Design: A Crazy Building in Columbus: Peter Eisenman', *Time*, 20 November 1989, p. 84; www.kurtandersen. com/journalism/time/a-crazy-building-in-columbus, accessed 30 March 2015.

87 Moneo, R., 'Unexpected Coincidences', in Moneo, R. & Vidler, A. (eds), *Wexner Centre for the Visual Arts, the Ohio State University*, New York: Rizzoli, 1989, p. 40. Also, Moneo, R., 'Unexpected Coincidences (Inesperadas Coincidencias)', *El Croquis* 41, 1989, p. 53.

88 Mayr, B., 'Architect Likes What He Sees at Wexner', *The Columbus Dispatch*, 1 November 2005, p. E3.

89 Moneo, 'Unexpected Coincidences', p. 40 (also p. 53); also, Bedard, op. cit., pp. 10–13.

90 www.wexarts.org/about/facilities/?path=/about/facilities/ mershon, accessed 20 November 2007.

91 Moneo, *Theoretical Anxiety*, p. 180.

92 Stearns, 'Building as Catalyst', in Moneo, R. & Vidler, A. (eds), *Wexner Centre for the Visual Arts, the Ohio State University*, New York: Rizzoli, 1989, p. 24.

93 Andersen, op. cit., p. 89; www.kurtandersen.com/journalism/ time/a-crazy-building-in-columbus, accessed 30 March 2015.

94 Sorkin, M., 'Solid Geometry', *House & Garden* 10/89, October 1989, p. 64.

95 Maymind, A., 'Still Ugly After All These Years: A Close Reading of

Peter Eisenman's Wexner Center', http://archinect.com/features/ article/49090085/still-ugly-after-all-these-years-a-close-reading- of-peter-eisenman-s-wexner-center, accessed 26 May 2014.

96 Bédard, J.-F., 'Introduction', and Eisenman, P. & Bédard, J.-F., 'Cannaregio: Submission to the International Seminar of Design for Cannaregio West, Venice, 1978', in Bédard, J.-F. (ed.), *Cities of Artificial Excavation: The Work of Peter Eisenman, 1978–1988*, Montreal and New York: Canadian Centre for Architecture & Rizzoli International, 1994, pp. 12–13 and pp. 46–71.

97 Jameson, F., 'Modernity Versus Postmodernity in Peter Eisenman', in Bédard, J.-F. (ed.), *Cities of Artificial Excavation: The Work of Peter Eisenman, 1978–1988*, Montreal and New York: Canadian Centre for Architecture & Rizzoli International, 1994, p. 31.

98 Eisenman, P. *with Balfour, A., Bédard, J.-F., Bois, Y.-A., Cohen, J.-F., Hays, M., & Olsberg, N.*, 'Conversations with Peter Eisenman', in Bédard, J.-F. (ed.), *Cities of Artificial Excavation: The Work of Peter Eisenman, 1978–1988*, Montreal and New York: Canadian Centre for Architecture & Rizzoli International, 1994, p. 119.

99 Ibid., p. 120.

100 Jameson, op. cit., pp. 34–35.

101 Leatherbarrow, *Topographical Stories*, p. 237.

102 Ibid., p. 236.

103 Moneo, 'Unexpected Coincidences', p. 41 (also p. 56).

104 Leatherbarrow, *Topographical Stories*, p. 237.

105 Ibid., pp. 237–239.

106 Moneo, 'Unexpected Coincidences', p. 41 (also p. 56).

107 Bosworth, A., 'A Building Waiting to be a Building', *The Columbus Monthly* 15, October 1989, p. 148.

108 Sorkin, op. cit., p. 65.

109 Ibid.

110 Vidler, A., 'Counter-Monuments in Practice: The Wexner Centre for the Visual Arts', in Moneo, R. & Vidler, A. (eds), *Wexner Centre for the Visual Arts, the Ohio State University*, New York: Rizzoli, 1989, p. 35.

111 Ibid., pp. 35–36.

112 Jameson, op. cit., p. 32.

100   Enis Aldallal | Site and Composition: Design strategies
Husam AlWaer and | in architecture and urbanism
Soumyen Bandyopadhyay |

113 Ibid., p. 33.

114 Eisenman, P., 'Wexner Centre', *El Croquis* 41, 1989, p. 30.

115 Dovey, op. cit., p. 47.

116 Leatherbarrow, *Topographical Stories*, p. 204.

117 Eisenman, P., 'Three Texts for Venice', in Bedard, J.-F. (ed.), *Cities of Artificial Excavation: The Work of Peter Eisenman, 1978–1988*, Montreal and New York: Canadian Centre for Architecture & Rizzoli International, 1994, p. 47.

118 Vidler, A., 'Counter-Monuments in Practice', in Moneo, R. & Vidler, A. (eds), *Wexner Centre for the Visual Arts, the Ohio State University*, New York: Rizzoli, 1989, p. 34.

119 Ibid., p. 33.

120 Moneo, 'Unexpected Coincidences', p. 56.

121 Leatherbarrow, *Topographical Stories*, p. 205.

122 Hartoonian, G., *The Crisis of the Object: The Architecture of Theatricality*, New York: Routledge, 2006, p. 51.

123 Eisenman, P., 'Cincinnati University', *El Croquis* 41, 1989, p. 105.

124 See Forster, K., 'Rising from the Land, Sinking into the Ground', in Davidson, C. (ed.), *Eleven Authors in Search of a Building*, New York: Monacelli Press, 1996, p. 116.

125 Barry, D., 'Connecting the Dots: The Dimensions of a Wire Frame', in Davidson, C. (ed.), *Eleven Authors in Search of a Building*, New York: Monacelli Press, 1996, p. 54.

126 Ibid., p. 55.

127 Ibid., p. 49.

128 Ibid.

129 Ibid.

130 Leatherbarrow, *Topographical Stories*, p. 48.

131 Forster, op. cit., p. 114.

132 Fredwest, J., http://daapspace4.daap.uc.edu/~larsongr/Larsonline/Eisenman_files/Eisen-DAAP.pdf, accessed 20 November 2007.

133 Barry, op. cit., p. 57.

134 Fredwest, op. cit., p. 5.

135 Leatherbarrow, *Uncommon Ground*, p. 183.

5 Enmeshed horizons: interior and exterior spaces

Michelangelo did not first conceive the inside of the basilica, then the outside, separately. He created the whole organism simultaneously.

Bruno Zevi[1]

In order to understand, it is immensely important for the person who understands to be located outside the object of his or her creative understanding. … Outsideness creates the possibility of dialogue, and dialogue helps us understand a culture in a profound way.

Mikhail Bakhtin[2]

While it is natural and necessary for architects to concentrate on the building itself, the bright light of this focus eclipses the surrounding world, darkening the very horizon that grants the building its standing.

David Leatherbarrow[3]

Introduction: space experience in architecture

No vacuum can be identified as a space if not registered with the corporeal experience. No architectural construct is spatial without an experience of it that encompasses both its interior and exterior, enabling the human body to experience a transitioning from the outside – from the space of the city – to the intimate spaces of the interior. In other words, a *void* can be called *space* only if accredited by our body and its entire system of senses (Figure 5.1). The experiential equilibrium, here, results from the reciprocity between the inside and the outside. Site as a socio-cultural construct – a positive fragment that contributes to and completes frameworks of spatialities – is part of a sequence of spaces connected through, often hierarchical but nonetheless communicative, spatial relationships.

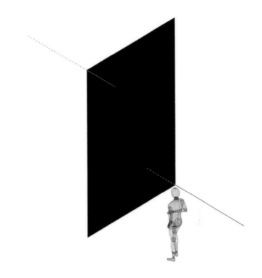

Figure 5.1 Man in space.

This chapter argues that to achieve an optimum integrity between site and context the spatial organisation of site should privilege the notion of sequential reciprocity between the interior of a building and its immediate exteriors, on the one hand, and between the site and its immediate vicinity, on the other. This calls for a closer examination of the term *in-between* – the boundary – as the common denominator distinguishing all such transitions. Balanced focus on the spatial settings of interiors and exteriors in any design approach entails giving equal attention to the *inside-out*, as well as the *outside-in* relationships. Examining the site simultaneously from inside-out and outside-in highlights and heightens our awareness of the binding socio-cultural constructs that resist isolation and autonomy, and enmesh both spaces and experiences.

To begin with, two important conceptions about architectural space need to be considered; together they form the fundamental ground on which the

104   Enis Aldallal | Site and Composition: Design strategies
Husam AlWaer and | in architecture and urbanism
Soumyen Bandyopadhyay

interrelationship of inside and outside is based. First, that space is a *void* unless defined by human bodily experience; and second, the interaction between the spatial fragment and the surrounding whole is sustained through ideas that help transform the perceptual properties of space into the concretised presence of architectural experience.

'There is no architectural space', Tschumi suggested, 'without something that happens in it, no space without content.'[4] To define a space through events that take place in it is intrinsic to its very character, as it implies engagement of the somatic with the actuality of architecture. Kant defined space as a property of mind, constructed within it, so that space exists as a pure intuition.[5] While this is fundamental in terms of observation, conception and projection, as elaborated in earlier chapters, in materialisation ideas enter into the realms of physical modes of representation. Spatial experience or *spatiality*,[6] therefore, not only involves the virtual, intangible qualities of space, but also those projected by materials and experienced or sensed, which makes the 'conceptual' space a tangible part of the 'corporeal' existence. The nature of space identified here, therefore, 'is not an abstract set of relations (nor an "ether") within which the life-world is structured. Rather, the lived experience of the body-in-space is the primary relation from which all conceptions of space are constructed.'[7] For Bruno Zevi, the spatial experience cannot be comprehended until the actual material expression has manifested the conceptual one through the human body by all means.[8]

Both the real and the virtual spaces have divergent manifestations not only in the domain of architecture but also in other disciplines such as painting, sculpture and filmmaking, some of which are planar while others are spatial. In most sculptures, for example, a spatial experience is generated when looked at from the outside. In painting, on the other hand, the spatial experience generated is ultimately limited by the planar qualities of the canvas. It is only architecture, however, that can provoke all the senses

and all the complexities of perception of the human body.[9] In architecture – analogous to a hollowed out sculpture and a series of overlapping canvasses – we apprehend the interior and exterior by moving through it, engaging fully through the dimension of time. Given that humans are both the subject and the object of architecture, to retain the experience of the event equally and continually on the inside and out, focus should be on integrating experiences into one meaningful continuum. For Zevi, the interpretation of architecture as space became meaningless and spatial experiences lost their legitimacy if two essential 'misunderstandings' about space were not removed. First, that 'architectural space can be experienced only in the interior of a building, and therefore urban or city-planned space, for all practical purposes, does not exist or have any value'. And second, 'space is not only the protagonist of architecture, but represents the *whole* of architectural experience, and that consequently the interpretation of a building in terms of space is the *only* critical tool required in judging architecture'.[10]

Spatial experience is reliant on the two mutually associated – yet independent – threads of visual and non-visual perception. They interrogate the boundaries of reality and truth, as Tschumi points out: 'Architecture constitutes the reality of experience while this reality gets in the way of … vision. Architecture constitutes the abstraction of absolute truth, while this very truth gets in the way of feeling.'[11] Feeling – as offered by the senses – can be considered the perceptive lenses of human interpretation of constructed space.[12] Zevi highlighted the three categories of spatial interpretation in architecture as content-based interpretation, formalistic interpretation and physio-psychological interpretation.[13] The lack of bodily experience of the 'architectural object' dismantles its adjectival essence and reduces it to a void where there is no sensible experience of event, light, material or detail. An example of this kind is the Greek temple, where the interiors were effectively voids, not spaces, for all the rituals and human experiences took place outside, in the open[14] (Figure 5.2),

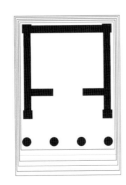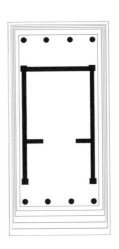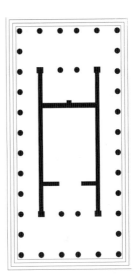

Figure 5.2 The Greek temple's inner void (after Trancik, R., 1986, *Finding Lost Space*).

which is also the case with the cuboidal structure at the centre of Islamic worship, the Ka'bah, where the cell-like interior is never open to experiencing. It is worth noting that, in defining architectural space, Rasmussen used the term *cavity* to refer to the limited, architecturally formed void, whereas he employed *space* to define the wider context allowing its foregrounding.[15]

In-between *chora*

To the ancient Greeks, however, both architectural space and reality were profound symbolisations of their Gods.[16] Hestia and Hermes represented 'a religious articulation of space and movement, of centre and path, of immutability and change'.[17] Hestia was a symbol of the earth, darkness and femininity and all qualities of 'interior space', whereas Hermes symbolised openness and contact with the outside – qualities associated with the external, public spaces.[18] However, it was not until Plato that the Greek idea of space and its reality was definitively articulated.

For Plato, to enter the human realisation of space, reality must have three components, which establish the bases for the communication with space – *being, becoming* and *chora*.[19] The first two entities clearly deal with object-like properties that have the qualification to form a tangible space. The *chora*, on the other hand, is something that has a dream-like, imaginal quality: an abstract characteristic of space that is both omnipresent and metaphysical.[20] Zevi's 'content-based' spatial properties thus parallel Plato's *being*, the 'formalistic' aligns with the *becoming*, and the 'physio-psychological' parallels the condition of the *chora*.

Defining the nature of the *chora* assumes importance in the context of our fragment–whole paradigm. First, it could refer to those key imaginal (virtual) qualities of space that underscore materialisation of space; and second, it could refer to thresholds or boundaries that define the sequential spatial transitions between inside and outside. For Plato, the *chora* lacks identity of its own as it always falls between the real and the ideal. Thus *chora* is also the ground that

106   Enis Aldallal | Site and Composition: Design strategies
         Husam AlWaer and | in architecture and urbanism
    Soumyen Bandyopadhyay |

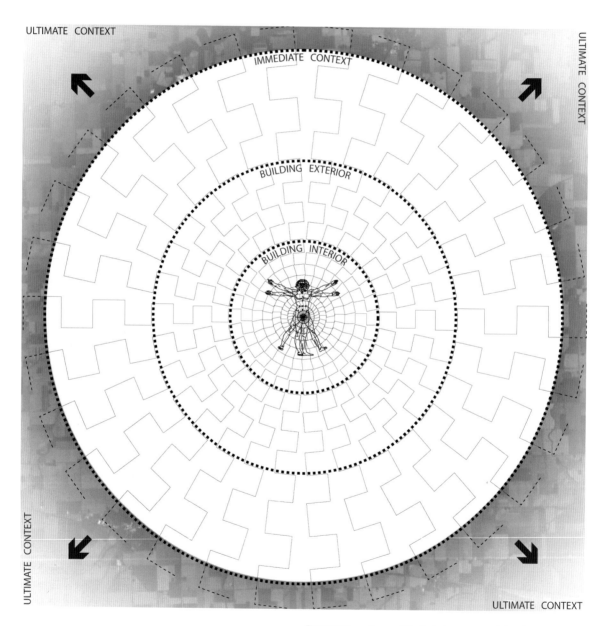

Figure 5.3 Boundary and the in-between space (*chora*).

allows the process of transformation from the conceptuality of drawing to the materiality of building. The property of space involves two interconnected references: a property of enclosure – corporeal (according to Semper) – and a property of mind – conceptual (according to Kant).[21] These references are framed within the coordinates of both space and time, which are not just a-priori mental or conceptual constructs but also corporeal ones, and whose counterparts are cultural and social forms of embodiments.[22] Hence, it is important to bear in mind that the virtuality of *chora* is, for sure, not limited to the arena of representation. This virtuality is an ingredient of what is real or what exists: 'the capacity of walls, boxes, windows, and corners to function in more than one way, to serve not only present functions but others as well, is already part of the ingenuity and innovation of the virtual in the real'.[23]

Architecture is not only defined through the inside and outside but also through the middle event – the *in-between*. While everyone would recall Venturi's maxim – architecture happens at the walls[24] – it is equally important to remind ourselves that 'it is no longer a sure thing that architecture takes place in walls, since walls no longer constitute a clear division between the interior and the exterior';[25] and that even the 'site is best viewed from points in between'.[26] To further underpin the reciprocal dialogue between the fragment and the whole, we aim to consider the event of the in-between (the boundary) – the *chora*, where the transformational mediation of programme and space takes place. Already, in previous chapters, we have highlighted the boundary as the 'communicative space', that is, the space that harbours the transitional movements and spatial overlaps from the smallest brush strokes of a painting to the artefacts of a city.

The in-between spaces carry divergent implications according to the locations they occupy; they perform divergent roles according to their scale and articulation, segregating architectural sequences – the inside, the building, the outside and the context (Figure 5.3).

Further, they possess the ability to change the apparently contradictory relationship between site and context, public and private, and the particular into an unexpected reciprocity.[27] The public is always open to external scrutiny, whereas the private is a shelter of life defined by one's family and friends. The particular articulates a higher level of intimacy that defines a particular event in a particular place and space. Between these entities Tschumi identified three categories of sequences: 'First, an internal relation, which deals with the method of work; then two external relations – one dealing with the juxtapositions of actual spaces, the other with program (occurrence or events).'[28] Venturi defined the in-between as 'residual space',[29] and further distinguished between *closed* and *open* residual spaces; to him these were the results of overlapping enclosures – enclosures within enclosures, serving as thresholds between what is on the perimeter and what is at the centre. He also argued that the closed were subordinate to those that were open, since in the process of making the architectural sentence the former were neither experienced nor apparent, while the open ones were engaged in that process and thus they were essential and dominant. However, the reduction in importance of the closed ones was, in fact, a reduction of their connective role between the dominant ones. Merleau-Ponty described the in-between as something less tangible but more phenomenological in nature. He described it as the 'ground' on which universal things can be brought together and could rest,[30] suggesting a possible intersection between his vision of the in-between and Plato's *chora*.

Continuities, reciprocities or displacements imply sequences and/or disjunctions of space/event/movement, on which the meaning of any architectural situation is dependent.[31] The purpose of the in-between, therefore, is critical in aiding spatial reciprocity; being in a state of perpetual construction and becoming, the *choric space* is directional – simultaneously constructing defined relationships, both outside-in, as well as inside-out. A choric space has the

108   Enis Aldallal | Site and Composition: Design strategies
Husam AlWaer and | in architecture and urbanism
Soumyen Bandyopadhyay ▮

ability to articulate the transitional shifts between the interior, the building, the exterior and the context, providing the shared ground where the conflicting/divergent polarities could interweave.

Reciprocity and disjunction versus convergence or stasis versus flow

Key to the interplay between the inside and the outside of an organ, the human body, a system or architecture is the physical skin that distinguishes them from their surroundings. In *The Shape of Touch* Pallasmaa explores the profound parallels between body and home, and the protective warmth ensured by the skin and the building enclosure, that fill the human psyche with comfort and intimacy. Through the skin our bodies are not only open biologically to their surroundings but also psychologically, socially and culturally. In this sense our bodies are permeable – porous and incomplete on their own[32] – which draws attention to the extant *reciprocity* between bodies and their surroundings. Thus architecture's role in fulfilling the analogous relationship between body and building – by addressing the reciprocity between inside and outside – is significant. Equally, for a site to act as a positive, interactive fragment (see Chapter 3), reciprocity needs to be given careful consideration.

Reciprocity, performed by the syntheses of spaces or actions, is about sequential enclosures and disclosures that bring the outside-in and the inside-out; the outside and the inside are transmutable, as if one includes the other. Sequential spaces articulate the relationship between inside and outside in terms of time, programme and juxtapositions. Reciprocal relationships between different spatial entities, therefore, are articulated through events or human actions that render tangible this relationship. Venturi elaborated this event as the *convergence* of both exterior and interior forces of use and space[33] and as the record of spatial overlaps. On the scale of an individual site a building can include spaces within spaces and enclosures within

enclosures, which open the door to interaction between series of internal and external worlds.

Elizabeth Grosz argues that it is not the convergence but the *disjunction* of spatial sequences through which the outside is active in the production of the inside.[34] However, given that space in its very nature is also continuous, conflict or indifference does not necessarily characterise reciprocity, but resolution and reinforcement – a mutual relationship between inside and outside. Convergence or disjunction operates through the perpetual reconfiguration of sites in terms of delineation, space, surface, movement, stasis, flow and so on. This is where the play is enacted between the fragmentary quality of the architectural site and its wider surroundings; the site bears the capacity and provision of a mediating existence that is in a perpetual state of *becoming* through its character as a *chora*.

The evolutionary vision of site, a sustainable and ever-changing position, hinges on two aspects of continuity or flow: first, the formal, compositional continuity between inside and outside; and second – resulting from the first – the constant growth and decline resulting from the materialisation of the architectural object. Hence, reciprocity of the inside and outside is defined by both the *chora* and its defining topography, keeping the human events in constant reciprocity, as far as the spaces could accommodate. This notion gains in strength as long as the site remains open to evolution, i.e. retains its continued ability to receive and include rather than to reject and exclude.

Speaking of polarities – inside/outside, private/public and stasis/flow – provokes the understanding of architecture as a series of contradictions, oppositions or conflicts. The existence of such polarities does not require choosing one over the other; rather, architecture has to oscillate between these poles, accelerating their mutual reciprocity, maximising their conflicting status or even signifying their indifference towards each other. Fixity of action and stasis are in fact manifestations of disjunction of sequence of both events and spaces, a condition identified by Thom Mayne as characterising the contemporary city: 'the physical manifestation of these destabilizing forces is that our contemporary cities are no longer identifiable as entities. A coherency of place (order) is lost as is the perceptibility of an edge or boundary.'[35] Making manifest the latent order addresses the morphology of a place, ensuring its continued coherency.

In Venturi's view, the continuity presented in Renaissance architecture had taken a formal rather than a compositional mode, as far as space was concerned. The continuity of mouldings, cornices, ornaments and pilasters in scale as well as material – found in churches and cathedrals – from inside to the outside, signalled the notion of flow.[36] A similar sort of contemporary compositional and tectonic continuity is found in Eisenman's Aronoff Centre for the Arts (1996; see Chapters 3 and 4; Figure 5.4). Referring to plate tectonics,

Figure 5.4 (above and overleaf) Peter Eisenman. The Aronoff Centre for the Arts, University of Cincinnati, Cincinnati, Ohio: the tectonic, ornamental continuation.

110

Enis Aldallal
Husam AlWaer and
Soumyen Bandyopadhyay

Site and Composition: Design strategies
in architecture and urbanism

to drifting, rocking and pulsing, Eisenman envisaged this building as 'nature systemic, systematic, rhythmical, dynamic – and hence inherently decorative or ornamental'.[37]

The notion of flow and continuity expressed by the early modern movement was often more passionately proclaimed than manifested by its protagonists. Apart from Wright's Prairie style houses and those designed by Loos, the early modern works contemplated especially by Le Corbusier and Mies van der Rohe engendered disjunction rather than continuity. In spite of developing significant architectural vocabularies, their buildings remained autonomous – formally, spatially and culturally – emanating stasis, not flow. The claimed flow between inside and outside, by substituting the conventional solid walls for window walls, for example, remained imperfect solutions – products of an over-simplistic understanding of spatial continuity. At the Glass House of Philip Johnson and at Mies' Barcelona Pavilion, the move creating a utilitarian core that supposedly accelerated the sense of openness and transition between the living spaces and the outside was ineffectual, as the glass curtain became an inactive accent within dominant openness.[38] Aldo van Eyck called it the modern 'sicknesses' of spatial continuity;[39] to him the transition between inside and outside should be articulated through well-defined in-between configurations that should not imply continual open sequences and endless postponements of progression between inside and outside. While largely remaining object buildings, Le Corbusier's post-Second World War works in India exhibit a critical understanding of both spatial and historical continuity, anticipating well in advance significant strands of postmodern thinking.

In reaction to modernist disjunction, postmodernism represented by its writer-architects – Aldo Rossi, Robert Venturi, Michael Graves and others – envisaged the recovery of historical continuity in a picturesque solution. Already Norberg-Schulz had called for an architecture that was interpreted through two major aspects: 'An architecture

which is determined by the need for physical milieu ... utilitarian, while an architecture determined by the need for symbol-milieu ... monumental.'[40] In Graves' view, the crisis of the modern movement was not only a historic one but also one of maintaining the cultural continuum.[41] The formal, picturesque historiography of the postmodern movement, however, entrapped itself in the futility of the recovery of the historical image, disjoining architecture from its role in the present and the future: '[w]e cannot rely on any kind of convention', Rykwert once emphasised, 'the world of tangible "form" has to be learnt anew'.[42]

Eisenman's work of the 1980s aimed to distinguish itself from postmodern conventions by employing strategies of artificial recovery (see Chapter 1). Tschumi echoed Eisenman's sentiments for retrieving the fictional archaeology of a site when he asserted that 'architectural sequences do not mean only the reality of actual buildings, or the symbolic reality of their functions. An implied narrative is always there, whether of method, use, or form.'[43] At Eisenman's Wexner Centre, for example, ideas of flow and sequence take on complex articulation through the scaffold and grids, which explores the potential of the *chora* as liminal space. Such articulation not only hinges on the formal, compositional and aesthetic considerations, but also on ensuring cultural accord. The former can be considered as the basis for the latter, or in other words as a tool to achieve cultural continuity. The solutions are often characterised by a fractured nature and fragmentary quality that provide a perpetual unfinished property to the projects.[44] This we discuss later with regard to Le Corbusier's Mill Owners' Association Building in Ahmedabad, India.

In constant search of new and redemptive forms, contemporary architecture, represented by a new *avant-garde*, not only adopted the trends illustrated above but reviewed, re-envisaged and reproduced them laced with the influence of both linguistics and the fine arts – painting and sculpture, in the main. These architects have employed the phenomenon of fragmentation, once so emphatically

112   Enis Aldallal | Site and Composition: Design strategies
Husam AlWaer and | in architecture and urbanism
Soumyen Bandyopadhyay |

championed by the Cubists, as a countermeasure to
remedy the disjunction engendered through modernism
and postmodernism. Zaha Hadid, a key member of this
group, once claimed that the task of contemporary
architecture is to discover the territories of the modern
movement that have not yet been discovered.[45] However,
what precisely this discovery might entail has remained
unclear. Grassi is correct in suggesting that 'for architecture
today to enter, in a real sense, into conflict with the cultural
superstructure according to which it is judged, it must be
unambiguous, to the point of didacticism, and not vague
or indistinct'.[46] Much of their work, conceived through
highly sophisticated drawings, paintings and ambiguous
diagrams, has created an autonomous world offering few
means of interpretation into real buildings, other than a
literal translation. As Eisenman's claim that architecture
does not solve problems, architecture creates problems[47]
would suggest, this new *avant-garde* appear to have set
themselves the task of solving false problems.[48] Admittedly,
the objective of the architectural endeavour is not to solve
all of humanity's problems, as Rykwert once observed,[49]
but equally its mission is not to plunge into a solipsistic
exercise in representation.

Libeskind suggested that his work 'in search of architecture
has discovered … no constant form and no universal
type…. Architecture is neither on the inside nor the outside.
It is not a given nor a physical fact.'[50] The contemporary
avant-garde's largely unsubstantiated rhetorical and, at
best, theoretical claims of continuity have in reality made
their architecture manifest disjunction and fragmentation
instead of flow and continuity. Such approaches have
given rise to the shredded, fragmented body of Gehry's Jay
Pritzker Pavilion (2004) at the Millennium Park in Chicago
or Coop Himmelblau's Falkestrasse in Vienna (1988) that are
made up of 'lifeless forms bringing together fragmentary
body parts in a kind of anatomical Lego game' (Figure 5.5).[51]
The suggestion is not to impose any universal type but a
sensitive situational elaboration, in which the site and the
building present significant opportunities of alignment

with both context and culture. A method that addresses the
constant interaction between the inside and the outside
would greatly impact on both the formal language of
architecture, as well as on its experience.

The defining horizon

A simple example of an architectural device aiding spatial
reciprocity is the Venetian window type, as Norberg-Schulz
describes, usually located on the corners of a room, which
makes visible the water reflections of the canals against the
walls.[52] There, the distinction between inside and outside
was not dismantled; rather, the condition was reinforced
through the introduction of window walls, projecting slabs,
cantilevers, transparencies and stratifications, making the
positioning of the window an implicit response to a specific
exterior circumstance. The 'destroyed box' of Wright was
among the earliest modern manifestations of bringing the
natural environment in. Between the Venetian window,
Wright's destroyed box and the window walls of Mies, the
reciprocity between the inside and the outside exhibited
diverse relationships. These varied from an expression
of formal openness towards the outside, to much more
carefully constructed – and deeper – manifestations of
welcoming the outside atmosphere, ushering the distinct
sense of place into the inside.

Figure 5.5 Frank Gehry. Jay Pritzker Pavilion, Chicago, Illinois: the
sculptural and fragmented structure of the pavilion.

At Alvaro Siza's Galician Centre for Contemporary Art in Santiago de Compostela, spatial reciprocity has been given substantial manifestation. An implicit, perspectival relationship between the museum, its interiors and its surrounding urban landscape, especially with the medieval cathedral, underpins the design.[53] Through an inverted window created by the wedge-shaped alignment of the external walls, the museum draws within it the presence of the cathedral. By responding to adjacent topographical features through the alignment of walls and boundaries of the surroundings with those of the building, the internal spatial arrangement acknowledges the outside, granting the museum a unique experience from inside-out and *vice versa*. Framed within the hollowed-out sculptural entrance porch, the ramp and the staircase provide access into the building, extending in the stratigraphy of the surrounding site and the approaches formed by pathways and steps. A further realignment inside the gallery congeals ramps and staircases into a formal axis of movement.

From the interior space of the Galician Centre to the urban space of the city, thresholds (choric spaces) mark transitions. These thresholds help distinguish yet interrelate the different events of architecture and history in the city. For Plato, *chora* is a strange condition of being or transitional construct. It is a space without

concrete boundaries, without identity of its own. It is a recipient, collective space, which takes from the outside to preserve the identity of inner spaces. The porosity and permeability of boundaries – building envelope, property boundary, immediate context and regional context – define sequences of events – of being and becoming – that characterise and make perceptible interior and exterior spaces through differing scales of concretisation. The location of choric space is always reliant on the position of observer/perceiver – all placed, in turn, within the encompassing physical and cultural topography. Thus, 'The consequence of these more concrete continuities between the interiors and their landscape setting', as Leatherbarrow elaborated, 'was that architectural design was discovered to be an art of articulating *topography*, its continuities, reciprocities, and displacements.'[54]

Architecture forms a small part of this embracing topography. Two interdependent aspects of movement could be envisaged: first, the flow *of* landscape – that of site – in its wider vicinity; and second, the flow of bodies as objects *in* the landscape. Since the somatic experience of space is guided and conceived by the sequences of spaces and enclosures through the dimension of time, topographic *horizons* or their perceived extents define this movement or flow. A building's context is the horizon of the building's

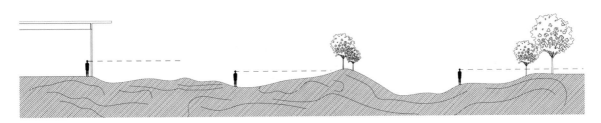

Figure 5.6 The *chora* and the defining horizon – topography.

114　　　　Enis Aldallal | Site and Composition: Design strategies
　　　　Husam AlWaer and | in architecture and urbanism
Soumyen Bandyopadhyay |

exterior, which is the horizon of the building, which in turn again is the horizon of the interiors (Figure 5.6).

The role of the in-between *chora* as a reconciliatory medium for the meeting of object and field is central to expressing the cultural topography and for strengthening the experience of place and identity. As already discussed (see Chapter 4), at the Wexner Centre the architecture meets diverse and distant horizons – the 'prairies' and the 'Jeffersonian grid', for example – through the landscaping of its forecourt (Figure 5.7).[55] The presence of the regional plantation, the grid and the pathways make simultaneous references to the immediate and the more distant horizons. How materiality in architecture could make references to both local and regional horizons will be discussed in Chapter 6.

The spatial experience our bodies undergo as we move from our personal space to the collective space and *vice versa* provides the essential basis for place-making. On the

inside we are inhabitants, whereas on the outside we are spectators. On the outside we are more open to changes informed by a broader consciousness of what surrounds us. Due to the implied opposition between the particular (inside) and the general (outside), architecture manifests different experiences and thereby suggests differing intellectual orientations toward the comprehension of the world. Such convictions have unfortunately led many designers to split sharply and radically their design approaches between the inside and the outside, instead of treating these as co-dependent entities. This, in turn, has not only created artificial disciplinary divisions such as *architecture* and *landscape architecture*, it has also given rise to much divided thinking characterising architecture either as *art* or as an exercise in narrow *functionalism*.[56]

Certain modern movement architects followed such assumptions, developing their architecture in relative detachment following the dictum 'from within to without', privileging use, ergonomics and instrumental spatiality,

Figure 5.7 Peter Eisenman. The Wexner Centre for the Visual Arts, Ohio State University, Columbus, Ohio: north-east forecourt (*chora*), a spatial experience referring to the Prairie landscape.

on the one hand, and form and aesthetic appearance, on the other. This resulted in added emphasis on Cartesian abstraction detaching architecture from the body, matter and feeling.[57] Decades later the postmodernists tried to fix this by referring to the outside solely through representational means, resulting in further detachment. The contemporary experimentations emphasising formal play and further – largely solipsistic – conceptual abstraction have exacerbated the gap between the physical and the sensual essence of architecture.[58] Also, the sensual relationship between body and building, established at the onset of the design process through the contact between the hand and the pencil, has been replaced by digital means of production. The contemporary architects are, as Frascari laments, 'happily and gruesomely clicking on the mouse at their workstations, these designers seek cockatrices, and produce behemoths'.[59] The detachment could be attributed to the anxiety among many architects to objectify their subjective and intuitive views into concretised resolution as soon as they have emerged.

When Wright destroyed the box at Robie House (Figure 5.8), it was done with the intention of inviting inwards the outside environment, both physically and perceptually. This was necessary to bring the light inside, engage materially with the surroundings, and to render tangible – by engaging all human senses – the spatial and material experiences between body and building. 'No concept of interior space alone', as Hoffmann wrote, 'could have resulted in such a transition, as Wright hinted when he wrote of the organic relation between exterior and interior. To an important extent the Robie house is shaped from the outside in.'[60] The poetic progression from outside inwards was described by Edgar Tafel when he visited the site with Mies van der Rohe and Wright: 'he had planned the visitor's progression … a whole architectural sequence, one event after another'.[61]

Aalto possessed a similar sensitivity towards achieving conjunction between outside and inside through space, materiality and especially through engagement of the

Figure 5.8 Frank L. Wright. Robie House, Chicago, Illinois: the inside-out/outside-in yard.

senses. While the modern machine culture, he observed, was giving people comfortable lives within their homes – technologically, the price paid for this was a certain disharmony.[62] The inside-out facilitates

> the emergence of what is hidden or obscured …
> it speaks of individual and collective experience
> because the process itself is the subject, because it
> includes people as well as time and space and place
> … it is tension because it is a search for balance
> among resources, needs, and purposes, because it is
> more than a participatory event: it is the struggle of
> new forms becoming manifest.[63]

By contrast, the outside-in is a collective effort, gathering the exterior forces that broaden the cosmic understandings of our consciousness. Aalto's Pension Institute in Helsinki, Asplund's Royal Chancellery in Stockholm and Stirling's Civic Centre Competition for Derby, are examples of this outside-in approach.

Charged fragments: reciprocity in Le Corbusier's Mill Owners' Association, Ahmedabad

Michel Jeanneret had suggested that the Renaissance was guided by a perpetual state of becoming, in which notions of the unfinished constituted a cultural

Figure 5.9 Le Corbusier. The Mill Owners' Association Building, Ahmedabad: facade.

condition for reinvention and rediscovery.[64] Such a cultural phenomenon has important implications far exceeding the particular worldview of the Renaissance, as a reading of Le Corbusier's Mill Owners' Association Building in Ahmedabad, India will aim to argue (Figure 5.9). Incomplete fragments were instrumental in the creation of a fused but porous whole, suggesting a strong reciprocity between the building fragments, its immediate site and wider cultural topography.

Corbusier's sketches during his Indian visits were complex fragments recording hitherto unencountered experiences, yet their incompleteness was replete with possibilities of connections. The extreme fragmented nature of his text entries, with suggestive connections codified in mathematical symbols (e.g. $+, -, =$), and the occasional underlined emphasis on phrases and words, created a multi-planar Cubist text, simultaneously finite and prosaic yet evocative and poetic, liberating space from the confines of stagnant words,[65] making it difficult not to misread the most prosaic of entries as poetic text.[66] Of particular interest is the manner in which Le Corbusier strove assiduously to reconcile the quasi-mythical with the mathematically charged fragments to arrive at a unique encompassing poetic whole, as if the latter was the result of a mysterious alchemical transformation.[67]

Equally engaging was his treatment of the architectural 'image' appropriate for the newly independent country, where he sought to embody the ambition of the future in the 'incomplete'. While arguably such a conception emerged out of an enduring presence in his mind of the Acropolis and the Indian ruins, a crucial distinction lay in the fact that the idea underpinned architectural evocations for a future, perhaps affirming Vladimir Nabokov's view that 'the future is but the obsolete in reverse'.[68] Together with the conscious employment of fragments, his Ahmedabad projects made use of the conception of the ruin as a powerful expression of a new future, created by collapsing and fusing the past and the future into a single space of a seemingly entropy-defying present.[69] By disrupting our longing for completeness, the incomplete holds within itself both an enhanced indication of what it could become, a result of our mind's projective cast into the future, as well as a sense that it has always been.

Porosity

The Ahmedabad projects express diverse notions of the ruin. The *brise soleil* appears to have its early manifestation – so it has been suggested – in the unfulfilled Carthage project of 1928.[70] Paradoxically, it is in his observation of life of the Indian poor that we detect its other origin, in an

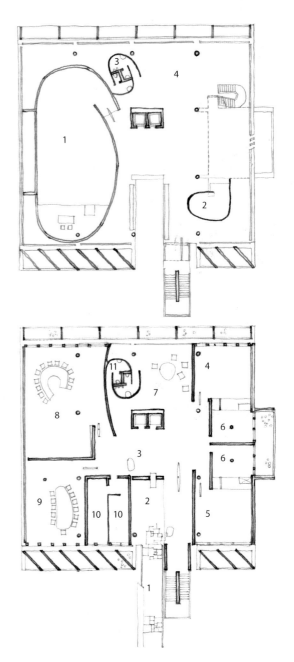

Figure 5.10 The Mill Owners' Association: plans (after *Global Architecture 37*); (a) entrance level: (1) Ramp, (2) entrance hall, (3) reception, (4) president's office, (5) vice president's room, (6) waiting area, (7) sub-committee room, (8) meeting room, (9) managing committee room, (10) office, (11) toilets. (b) Upper level: (1) meeting room, (2) cloakroom, (3) toilets, (4) lobby.

118 Enis Aldallal | Site and Composition: Design strategies
Husam AlWaer and | in architecture and urbanism
Soumyen Bandyopadhyay |

Figure 5.11 The Mill Owners' Association: entrance ramp and staircase.

artefact of everyday use nearing obsolescence: the tattered curtain. It provided the basis for the eight vibrant perforated tapestries of the High Court in Chandigarh (see Chapter 2), as well as the *brise soleil* in Ahmedabad. The connection – at least in Le Corbusier's mind – between the *brise soleil* and the fragile piece of fabric offering 'an Indian [brand of] Héraclite comfort',[71] points to the essentially 'extra-architectural' nature of the screen and parallels the origin of Indian architecture itself, in the rock-cut Buddhist cave temples of western India – in which Lutyens failed to find any architectural merit at all.

Mill Owners' and Shodhan House are overt embodiments of this idea of the *brise soleil* as ruin, both exploring further how this condition weaves into, expands or even interrupts the day-to-day inhabitation of these buildings. At Mill Owners' (Figures 5.10–5.13) the facade breaks down – as hewn-out mass from the building's cuboid form is displaced outside – to create a rusticated, cavernous zone of transition, made even more rugged through the strong Ahmedabad sun. It recalls the dark hollow beaconing of elaborate entrances of rock-cut cave temples; at Karle, for example, nature and the essentially incomplete character of human intervention overlap, fused further by the play of light, a quality the early Romantic etchings so appropriately captured.[72] Equally Romantic is Le Corbusier's Mill Owners', for not only does his screen anticipate a gradual reclamation by nature (through the growth of vegetation within the *brise soleil* plant beds), but it itself displays the paradoxical qualities of fragility, but also depth and density (Figures 5.14 and 5.15). Considering the building outside-in, the formal ambiguity of the building's membrane and vegetation

suggests the emergence of a choric space of event, where the natural landscape kept at bay by the expanding city is drawn into dialogue with the materiality of the building.

Beyond, a vertical concrete plane deliberately obstructs direct view by rising through the double-height entrance space, with a rectilinear aperture positioned along the centre line of the ramp that leads up to the entrance, forcing a visitor to re-orient themself to access the central space.

Figures 5.12–5.13 Mill Owners' Association: the breakdown of facade as 'hewn-out' mass from the building's cuboid form is displaced outside to form a staircase.

120   Enis Aldallal | Site and Composition: Design strategies
Husam AlWaer and | in architecture and urbanism
Soumyen Bandyopadhyay |

Figures 5.14–5.15 The Mill Owners' Association: deep planters within the *brise soleil* and the gradual reclamation by nature of the rear facade.

The orthogonal geometry set up by the facade extends inwards, flanking this space, which overlooks the river from an elevation. Another screen – a much shallower and more delicate one – frames the view of the River Sabarmati (Figures 5.16 and 5.17). Together with what Frampton called the upper level 'minstrels gallery',[73] the space recalls Kailasha, Cave XVI in Ellora, a representation of the celestial abode of Lord Shiva. In being lifted up the ramp and drawn into the central space one is transformed into an object of ritual offering to the river, a holy rite practised on the banks of Indian rivers. To understand how precisely the redemptive space functions, one has to look into the role played by the ramp and the vertical plane, which we would argue plays a key role in a topographic fabrication that attempts to reconcile the opposition of nature and the man-made. Congealed within the porosity of the facades are diverse cultural horizons separated in time and space.

Fragments

The treatment of this theme of the 'inhabited ruin' extends inwards through the spatial organisation. The central space consists of a series of curvilinear fragments or situated moments, orchestrated around the orthogonal presence of a monolithic lift core. The three curvilinear elements are the reception desk, the table in the waiting area and, finally,

implicit in the phallic representation of Lord Śiva.[74] That the 'churning rod' was a conscious conception is clear from its projection above the roof plane; this *axis mundi* appears to be held in place by the ground (which also includes the ground floor, below the main entrance space, invisible and subordinated through its 'servant' programme). At roof level, a curious juxtaposition of the extended column and the projected incline of the conference hall roof also lends itself to a more prosaic reading of this central feature: that of a fragment of a giant machine – perhaps wheels of a water mill or a spindle associated with the textile industry, the *raison d'être* for the Mill Owners' – positioned carefully in proximity to the river (Figure 5.19).[75] While this device and the floor plans indicate Le Corbusier's continued fascination with interiors as discreet arrangement of equipment,[76] which, given his fascination with the rivers of India and notions of purity and sanctity,[77] will have been employed with a purificatory intent; one is reminded of the creation myth associated with Lord Śiva – *neelakantha*, the one with a blue throat – who drank the venom to clarify the nectar. At Mill Owners' we are therefore presented with both a prosaic icon of productivity that lay at the heart of the city's wealth creation and a profound creative allusion, and the results (or products) of such actions. The cusped toilets, therefore, could be seen to be the key embryonic implantation instigating the reversal of obsolescence, contributing to the Indian project of *renovatio*.

the interlocking curved walls holding between them the male and female toilets – a delicate, perhaps precarious embryonic adhesion to the voluptuous female body of the conference hall (Figure 5.18; see Figure 5.10). While the tables designed in the manner of the roof cut-outs are indeed microcosmic representations, the male–female union is indicative of two crucial mytho-religious themes: the creation myths relating to the churning (*manthana*) of the eternal sea that brought forth the nectar using the mythical serpents as the churning chord, and the penetrative union of the *linga* (phallus) and the *jyoni* (vagina)

122　　Enis Aldallal | Site and Composition: Design strategies
　　　Husam AlWaer and | in architecture and urbanism
　Soumyen Bandyopadhyay |

Figures 5.16–5.17 The Mill Owners' Association (previous page): framed view of the Sabarmati River through the rear facade (above).

Reciprocal construction of site

The mediating role of the vertical plane positioned at the entrance is further articulated by the aperture set within it, with its projected ledge focusing down the ramp (Figure 5.20). Through this ingenious device the ritual passage turns back on itself to re-orient away from the river, towards the city. The redemptive role of the central space with its mytho-religiously charged fragments is completed by the implied issuing forth of the nectar through this 'spout', embedded within which is the reconciled duality of purity and impurity (of water). Only now can one comprehend the pivotal role of his recordings of the 'water mill' of Amritsar or the aerial view of the sloping track for drawing water.[78] It has been argued how the interior of the building, with its stone-faced walls, stands in contrast to the bold ruggedness of the exterior concrete.[79] The hand-finished paving slabs on the ramp, as well as the paving on the ground beyond, pick up the order of the interior stone facing and appear to bring it down in

one uninterrupted fluid flow, a theme that also features in his treatment of the water channel in Shodhan House, which runs down from the roof in conjunction with a staircase, echoing the relationship between these two elements at the Mill Owners'. The building's obsolescence is perpetuated by a questioning – perhaps even subversive – employment of programme, which expands its monumentality. The prominent positioning of the toilets cusped between the erotic curvatures within the main space interrogates the spatial hierarchy of served and servant spaces. To an extent, the move renders the surrounding programme obsolete, flushed out, as it were, with the flow. Significantly, in the unbuilt site plan proposal the relationship between orthogonal and curvilinear elements found inside the building was reversed in the exterior landscape (Figure 5.21). Within the building, curvilinear elements are held in place by an orthogonal grid arrangement; this is reversed in the landscape proposal, where diagonally placed orthogonal servant quarters and guard houses – with curvilinear

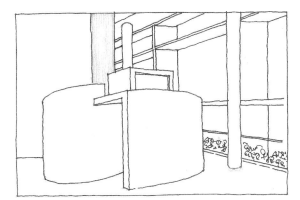

its site at the Mill Owners', employing and manipulating a simple, instrumental opposition, Le Corbusier not only grounds the building within its site but also constructs a site out of virgin development by firmly establishing its relationship as a fragment to a wider whole. The building's ability to bring together – yet question – diverse cultural horizons, is remarkable.

Conclusion: the residual mission of site

Intimacy versus formality, and subjective versus objective, are driving forces of human innovation. Without the subjectivity (thinking from inside) it would have been a world of banal manifestations and repetitive production. Without the objectivity (thinking from outside), on the other hand, this world would be a chaotic place of personal statements and self-centric ideologies. Architecture has the ability to render visible and make experiential all such dialectics.

This chapter began with the suggestion that a legitimate architectural experience of space is subject to a culturally conditioned bodily understanding of inside and outside. The site was seen as a set of hierarchical and sequential events and spaces – the interior, the building, the exterior

Figure 5.18 The Mill Owners' Association: interlocking curved walls housing the toilets.

adhesions similar to the Shodhan House servants' quarters – are contained within a pronounced curvilinear wall. Le Corbusier's employment of curvilinear and orthogonal orders to represent nature–culture or female–male is well known. In employing reciprocity between the building and

Figure 5.19 The Mill Owners' Association: roof detail with free-standing column and conference room roof.

124   Enis Aldallal | Site and Composition: Design strategies
        Husam AlWaer and | in architecture and urbanism
    Soumyen Bandyopadhyay |

Figure 5.20 The Mill Owners' Association: free-standing plane at the entrance with inset aperture and 'spout'.

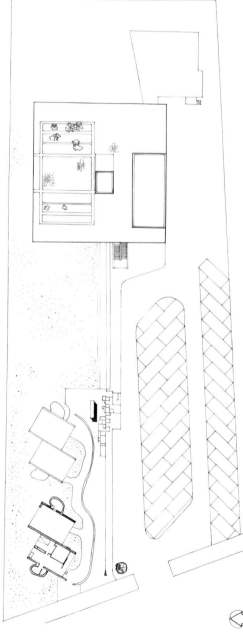

Figure 5.21 The Mill Owners' Association: site plan (after *Global Architecture* 37).

and the context – defined by the choric condition of the ambiguous in-between that is simultaneously defining and porous. It has the ability to transform the ideal aspects of space into the tangible. Each event is defined by the horizon of the former one in such a way that it contributes to hierarchical overlaps and movements between an 'inside' and its 'context'. Each horizon contains a terrain – an expansive cultural topography encompassing all human endeavour, overlapping with spatial experience. Topography is thus critical to the reciprocity between inside and outside – between those sequential events and experiences. Unifying the human experience of architectural space of inside and outside is an exercise in privileging the spatial experience of the architectural object by keeping the sense of place at its heart as the true generator. Pulling the inside out and bringing the outside in is not only a matter of installing window-walls that accelerate the sense of flow and visibility between them. It is a matter of simultaneously articulating boundaries between them, the in-between *chora*, an event that congeals our intimate, particular experiences, as well as our cosmic understanding. The positive-fragmentary quality of a site emerges from such profound collaboration between defining topographies and choric spaces.

126   Enis Aldallal | Site and Composition: Design strategies
Husam AlWaer and | in architecture and urbanism
Soumyen Bandyopadhyay |

Notes

1 Zevi, B., *Architecture as Space*, New York: Horizon, 1957, p. 51.

2 Morson, G. & Emerson, C., *Mikhail Bakhtin: Creation of a Prosaics*, Stanford, CA: Stanford University Press, 1990, p. 55.

3 Leatherbarrow, D., *Uncommon Ground: Architecture, Technology, and Topography*, Cambridge, MA: MIT Press, p. 170.

4 Tschumi, B., *Event-Cities 3*, Cambridge, MA: MIT Press, 2004, p. 11.

5 Forty, A., *Words and Buildings: A Vocabulary of Modern Architecture*, London: Thames & Hudson, 2000, p. 258.

6 For *spatiality*, see Leatherbarrow, D., *Architecture Oriented Otherwise*, New York: Princeton Architectural Press, 2009, p. 243.

7 Dovey, K. *Framing Places: Mediating Power in Built Form*, New York: Routledge, 1999, p. 39.

8 Zevi, op. cit., p. 29.

9 Holl, S., 'Questions of Perception: Phenomenology of Architecture', in Holl, S., Pallasmaa, J. & Pérez Gómez, A., *A+U: Questions of Perception: Phenomenology of Architecture*, San Francisco, CA: William Stout Publishers, 2007, p. 41.

10 Zevi, op. cit., p. 214.

11 Tschumi, B., *Architecture and Disjunction*, Cambridge, MA: MIT Press, 2004, p. 48.

12 Onians, J., 'Greek Temple and Greek Brain', in Dodds, G. & Tavernor, R. (eds), *Body and Building: Essays on the Changing Relationship of Body and Architecture*, Cambridge, MA: MIT Press, 2002, p. 45.

13 Zevi, op. cit., p. 214.

14 Ibid.

15 Rasmussen, E., *Experiencing Architecture*, London: Chapman & Hall, 1959, p. 48.

16 Pérez Gómez, A., 'The Space of Architecture: Meaning as Presence and Representation', in Holl, S., Pallasmaa, J. & Pérez Gómez, A., *A+U: Questions of Perception: Phenomenology of Architecture*, San Francisco, CA: William Stout Publishers, 2007, p. 13.

17 Ibid.

18 Ibid.

19 Ibid., p.12.

20 Ibid., p. 13.

21 Forty, op. cit., p. 258.

22 Grosz, E., *Architecture from the Outside: Essays on Virtual and Real Space*, Cambridge, MA: MIT Press, 2001, p. 32.

23 Ibid., p. 90.

24 Venturi, R., *Complexity and Contradiction in Architecture*, New York: Museum of Modern Art, 1966 (1977 reprint), p. 86.

25 Norberg-Schulz, C. (Nasso, C. & Parini, S., eds; Shugaar, A., trans.) *Architecture: Presence, Language and Place*, Milan: Skira, 2000, p. 317.

26 Burns, C. & Kahn, A., 'Introduction', in Burns, C. & Kahn, A. (eds), *Site Matters: Design Concepts, Histories and Strategies*, New York and Abingdon: Routledge, 2005, p. xxiii.

27 Tschumi, *Event-Cities 3*, p. 14.

28 Tschumi, *Architecture and Disjunction*, p. 153.

29 Venturi, op. cit., p. 80.

30 Holl, citing Merleau-Ponty, 'Questions of Perception', p. 45.

31 See, for example, Tschumi, *Architecture and Disjunction*, p. 162.

32 Franck, K. & Lepori, B., *Architecture from the Inside Out: From the Body, the Senses, the Site, and the Community*, London: Wiley Academy, 2007, p. 48.

33 Venturi, op. cit., p. 86.

34 Grosz, op. cit., p. 68.

35 Mayne, T., 'Connected Isolation', in Jencks, C. & Kropf, K. (eds), *Theories and Manifestoes of Contemporary Architecture* (second edition), London: Wiley Academy, 2006, p. 301.

36 Venturi, op. cit., p. 70.

37 Cobb, H., 'A Note on the Criminology of Ornament: From Sullivan to Eisenman', in Davidson, C., *Eleven Authors in Search of a Building*, New York: Monacelli Press, 1996, p. 97.

38 Venturi, op. cit., p. 82.

39 Ibid., p.80.

40 Norberg-Schulz, C., *Intentions in Architecture*, Cambridge, MA: MIT Press, 1965, p. 185.

41 Graves, M., 'A Case for Figurative Architecture', in Jencks, C. & Kropf, K. (eds), *Theories and Manifestoes of Contemporary Architecture* (second edition), London: Wiley Academy, 2006, p. 93.

42 Rykwert, J., 'Ornament is no Crime', in Rykwert, J., *The Necessity of Artifice*, London: Academy Editions, 1982, p. 101.

43 Tschumi, *Architecture and Disjunction,* 1996, p. 163.

44 Mayne, op. cit., p. 302.

45 Hadid, Z., 'The Eighty-Nine Degrees', in Jencks, C. & Kropf, K. (eds), *Theories and Manifestoes of Contemporary Architecture* (second edition), London: Wiley Academy, 2006, p. 280.

46 Grassi, G., 'Avant-Garde and Continuity', in Hays, M. (ed.), *Oppositions Reader*, New York: Princeton Architectural Press, 1998, p. 393.

47 Eisenman, P., Lecture at the Aronoff Centre for the Arts, University of Cincinnati on the tenth anniversary of its inauguration, 2006.

48 Grassi, op. cit., p. 392.

49 Rykwert, J., 'The Necessity of Artifice', in Rykwert, J., *The Necessity of Artifice*, London: Academy Editions, 1982, p. 58.

50 Libeskind, D. 'Unoriginal Signs', in Jencks, C. & Kropf, K. (eds), *Theories and Manifestoes of Contemporary Architecture* (second edition), London: Wiley Academy, 2006, p. 281.

51 Frascari, M., 'A Tradition of Architectural Figures: A Search for Vita Beata', in Dodds, G. & Tavernor, R. (eds), *Body and Building: Essays on the Changing Relationship of Body and Architecture*, Cambridge, MA: MIT Press, 2002, p. 259.

52 Norberg-Schulz, *Architecture: Presence, Language and Place*, p. 163.

53 Temple, N., *Disclosing Horizons: Architecture, Perspective, and Redemptive Space*, London and New York: Routledge, 2007, pp. 150–159.

54 Leatherbarrow, *Uncommon Ground*, p. 176.

55 See Leatherbarrow, *Topographical Stories*, pp. 238–239.

56 Franck & Lepori, op. cit., p. 23.

57 Ibid., p. 154.

58 Pallasmaa, J., 'An Architecture of the Seven Senses', in Holl, S., Pallasmaa, J. & Pérez Gómez, A., *A+U: Questions of Perception: Phenomenology of Architecture*, San Francisco, CA: William Stout Publishers, 2007, p. 29.

59 Frascari, op. cit., p. 259.

60 Hoffmann, D., *Frank Lloyd Wright's Robie House: The Illustrated Story of an Architectural Masterpiece*, New York: Dover Publications, 1984, p. 44.

61 Ibid.

62 Schildt, G., *Alvar Aalto in His Own Words*, New York: Rizzoli, 1998, p. 150.

63 Franck & Lepori, op. cit., pp. 41–44.

64 Jeanneret, M., *Perpetual Motion: Transforming Shapes in the Renaissance from da Vinci to Montaigne*, Baltimore, MA: Johns Hopkins University Press, 2001, cited in Temple, N. & Bandyopadhyay, S., 'Contemplating the Unfinished', in Frascari, M., Hale, J. & Starkey, B. (eds), *From Models to Drawings: Imagination and Representation in Architecture*, London: Routledge, 2007, p. 110.

65 See, for example, Le Corbusier, *Le Corbusier Sketchbooks*, London: Thames & Hudson, 1981–2, Sketchbook F27, p. 895.

66 See, for example, ibid., a programme brief in Sketchbook F25, p. 806.

67 See, for example, ibid., Sketchbook F24, p. 700; also E23, p. 694 and F24, p. 756.

68 Flam, J. (ed.), *Robert Smithson: The Collected Writings*, Berkeley, CA: University of California, 1996, p. 11.

69 Ibid., pp. 10–23, 301–309.

70 Frampton, K., 'Le Corbusier and the Dialectical Imagination', *Global Architecture* 37, 1975, pp. 2–5.

71 Le Corbusier, op. cit., Sketchbook E18, p. 359.

72 See, for example, Ferguson, J. (Burgess, J. & Spiers, R., eds), *History of Indian and Eastern Architecture 1*, Delhi: Munshiram Monoharlal, 1876 (second Indian edition, 1972), p. 144 (fig. 69).

73 Frampton, op. cit., p. 4.

74 For an indication of his awareness, see Le Corbusier, op. cit., Sketchbook J36, p. 298.

75 Ibid., Sketchbook F24, p. 756.

128   Enis Aldallal | Site and Composition: Design strategies
Husam AlWaer and | in architecture and urbanism
Soumyen Bandyopadhyay |

76 Leatherbarrow, *Architecture Oriented Otherwise*, p. 136.

77 Le Corbusier, op. cit., Sketchbook E23 p. 26; J35, p. 222; J37, pp. 366, 368.

78 Ibid., Sketchbook H30, p. 1056 and E18, p. 346.

79 Frampton, op. cit., p. 4.

6 Materiality and the culture of place

The acknowledgment of new cultural pressures
and new materials was not to put an end to the
transmission of past practices but to serve as the
provocation for their renewal and redefinition.

David Leatherbarrow[1]

Introduction

During the past few years, especially but not exceptionally
within the pedagogic environment, the term *materiality*
has gained prominence in architectural discourse and
praxis. One can draw parallels between the performance
of *space*, *spaces* and *spatiality*, on the one hand, and
material, *materials* and *materiality*, on the other. Space and
material are both 'conceptual and universal', which can be
distinguished from spaces and materials, which are 'at once
particular and factual, known directly and immediately
as the fabric and framework of our lives'.[2] However,
like spatiality, materiality refers 'not to the phenomena
themselves but to one's experience and sense of them'.[3]
The employment of materials suggests decision-making;
considerations such as physical properties, availability,
aesthetics, environment and comfort, can be the basis for
material selection. Materiality, thus, mediates between the
conceptual and the concretised nature of architecture; it is
that which gives material architecture its relevance or makes
it meaningful.

An important source of materiality often misunderstood by
architects – but especially conservationists and planners
– is the contextual employment of materials to ensure
continuity with their immediate surroundings. Here,
instrumental thinking has generally prevailed in upholding
place identity, emphasising a literal continuity of material
use, supported by graphic and scalar analytical and
representational methods to demonstrate the building's
resistance to the threat of contextual and temporal rupture
posed by the process of design. This resistance, however,
can neither be achieved by literal continuity of image or the

ideogram, nor by self-referential compositions. For, if design
is seen as that ingenuous process of transformation that
conjoins anthropological demands (i.e. use, inhabitation,
history, culture and societal demands) with the site,
the relation between past and present could hardly be
regarded as being static. Instead, reconciling the conflicting
memories of the pre-existing and the aspirations of the
new by exploiting to the fullest the building's mediatory
role is the tool to achieve that resistance. Thus, discussion
in this chapter suggests that places are places before and
after the process of remaking the site has taken place
and the advent of the building; what matters are the
perceptual qualities of the material intervention in ensuring
anthropological and cultural continuity. Departure from
meaningful materialisation in architectural practice today
could be attributed to a number of reasons. Today, it is
not often that material selection takes into account site-
specific references, especially within a rapidly globalising
scene of architectural practice, which has removed much
of the cultural considerations of place. It has also widened
the chasm between occupants and buildings, on the one
hand, and sites and their wider built and natural context,
on the other. The consequent treatment of architecture as
autonomous object has eclipsed the capacities of elements
such as the building envelope to achieve meaningful
dialogue with context.

In order for the site to become an expressive spatial
experience that implies place identity, it should provoke
certain responses by means of its materiality that renders
the abstract tangible, for 'the experience of space is not
communicated until the actual mechanical expression has
rendered material the poetic conception'.[4] Looking at site
through different levels of totality is necessary to examine
its fragmentation (dissociation) versus the defragmentation
(connectedness) discussed in earlier chapters. Enmeshed
experiences considering material transformation between
parts and the whole identify the embracing role of
topography in siting practices. Indeed, discussions on
materiality in the nineteenth century have highlighted

132   Enis Aldallal | Site and Composition: Design strategies
Husam AlWaer and | in architecture and urbanism
Soumyen Bandyopadhyay

topography as the substantial source of material selection. The buildings studied in the following discussion will thus be defined by two topographical extensions: the *immediate* context (locale) and the *ultimate* context (region). Identifying those totalities without defining their boundaries – i.e. those constituent surfaces of site spatiality that distinguish and separate them – would be pointless. The purpose of introducing the term *boundaries* into this discussion is to highlight its role in what could be termed *material metabolism* in relation to the topography of a place. Material metabolism possesses the capacity for ensuring the site's continued relevance over time; boundary considerations bring in the idea of mediation into the collective material representation.

Place considerations: place between perception and materialisation

Materiality in architectural design could be seen as the projective relationship between drawing and building, between abstract conception and material manifestation; its significance lies in its alternation between eye/drawing relationship and body/building experience. Though existing as discrete stages, often separated chronologically from each other, the eye/drawing and body/building relationships highlight the acute interdependency between perception and materialisation.

The dematerialisation of the architectural object, originally championed by the modern movement but enhanced in the contemporary age of increasing globalisation of the architectural practice – the latter helped by technological advances in the fabrication of the building envelope – has, however, precipitated a crisis regarding its representational content and nature. The clash between the local and the global makes our place experience alternate between familiarity and unfamiliarity. These two terms impact not only on our perception of place but also on our judgement of it, which affects the form of intervention. Unless trained otherwise, as outsiders, acting as unfamiliar actors or

strangers, we have limited knowledge of the specificity of a place. Equally, as blasé insiders, too frequently exposed to place specificity, we become nonchalant, detached and even ignorant actors. The lack of attention to circumstance, therefore, can negatively affect the nature of place in significant ways. Dovey's view that our experience of place 'marks the beginning and the end of every architectural and urban design project',[5] i.e. the site is a midway station between place and place, is poignant here, a notion discussed in Chapter 4 in terms of projection. Sadly, the void created through disengagement with place is being filled by too many self-referential architectural objects.

The role of architecture, in many ways, is similar to that of place; they both crystallise the connection between life and a given ambient. Site materialises our interpretation of both place and life. While such interaction was examined spatially in Chapter 5, where site was defined as a social construct whose spatial setting addressed the overlap of actions, the present chapter will discuss aspects of material reciprocity. In Heidegger's view, the imaginative projection of a place involves linking up its material and anthropological aspects through us, thinking of its qualities, its memorable events, people associated with it and even the fictions made about it.[6] Pallasmaa, on the other hand, arguing for the need for a highly attuned sensitivity, has suggested that we regress back into our bodies – to include the skeleton and the muscles, besides our five senses – to establish a fully comprehensible experience of place.[7]

Intervening on-site as a place-making mission suggests linking its parts progressively to a whole that extends beyond the site itself. The 'identity of figures', as Norberg-Schulz suggests, 'is not in fact an absolute *idea*, but a manifestation of a way of being open'.[8] To retain place specificity, Gunnar Asplund treated each project individually; each had its own specificity and its own way of producing the details.[9] More recently, Zumthor's approach has paralleled Asplund's, who has addressed the anchoring of place by suggesting the collecting of memories and actions linked to it. 'It is essential to the quality of intervention', he elaborated, 'that the new building should embrace qualities which can enter into a meaningful dialogue with the existing situation. For if the intervention is to find its place, it must make us see what already exists in a new light.'[10] The material chosen could potentially influence both the form as well as the perception of a building; at the very least, emplacement can impact on a building's aesthetic qualities.[11]

The fragment–whole relationship thus raises the possibility of interaction between the pre-existing and the new, which suggests that what already exists is either proclaimed in the man-made work (i.e. through site and the architectural object), as evidenced in Zumthor's architecture, or that this work fills a gap identified in the surrounding environment.[12] An example of the latter is Richard Meier's Douglas House in Harbor Springs, Michigan (1973; Figure 6.1), which through its taut, white enclosure simultaneously disrupts the uniformity of the natural vegetation of its steeply sloping site, and introduces a device for viewing nature. As these examples indicate, this is not a call for a conservative, retrograde idealisation of place circumstance in the sense of a return to the primitive. Instead, it is a call for avoiding the dangers of superficiality brought on by interventions that address narrow personal architectural predilections, on the one hand, and the new tendencies towards universal uniformity posited by globalisation, on the other. Thinking of material selection in terms of place extension, thus, could constitute an important part of a renewed addressing of the sense of place, identity and interaction.

Place extension: immediate context, ultimate context and material invention

Ideas of place extension and their impact on site identity are embedded in Frampton's idea of *Critical Regionalism*,[13] where architecture simultaneously resists and mediates between the local/global pressures on a particular place. 'The fundamental strategy of Critical Regionalism',

Frampton suggested, 'is to mediate the impact of universal civilization with elements derived indirectly from the peculiarities of a particular place.'[14] Tensions of local/global, immediate/ultimate and so on, entail drawing careful attention to their meanings within specific cultural, spatial and material strategies and contexts of their appearance. Because material selection is always defined by context, the basis for such selection can be raised to review two conceptions of context: the *immediate context* – the locale – and the *ultimate context* – the region.

The *immediate context* or 'locale' is the set of places and spaces that directly surround the site and, hence, its impact on site is prompt, instantly drawing in the influence of place. The aggregation of 'locales' constitutes the second category – the *ultimate context* or region, which extends our perception of context to an even broader territory. That the siting of Douglas House could be considered both within an immediate context of a steeply sloping topography and dense foliage, and as part of the wider landscape of Lake Michigan, offers a simple example of the simultaneous existence of the two contexts.

Local materials or the influence of immediate context

Criteria for material selection, such as their properties, techniques of production and employment, durability, availability, and their architectural interest, are all decisive factors in architectural materialisation. These considerations alone, however, could potentially limit the ability of a material palette to express place identity. The selection of a certain local or non-local material could be subject to wider logistical constraints rather than the appreciation of the perceptual and anthropological qualities of place. Leatherbarrow's view that 'it was not always the case that all materials could be sent to all places',[15] while highlighting this obvious problem of material procurement, also alludes to a more important question of whether all materials *should* be sent to all places. Materials – their various

134   Enis Aldallal | Site and Composition: Design strategies
Husam AlWaer and | in architecture and urbanism
Soumyen Bandyopadhyay |

Figure 6.1 Richard Meier. Douglas House, Harbor Springs, Michigan: view from Lake Michigan.

qualities and properties – through their employment over centuries, have acquired specific meanings within defined contexts, and have therefore evolved as cultural assets. Familiar materials provide the context for unfamiliar material importations to exist and *vice versa*, suggesting the opportunity for the designer to speak through materiality. This ability to comment on the human and material condition at a given place and time – and at divergent levels of perception – is what removes material employment away from being a mere instrumental act into a deeply perceptual practice. As Rykwert aptly put it, it is the architect's comment on 'both action and material which regulates the surface of the artefact, and the very word "comment" in this context robs the architect or planner of any pretence at objectivity, in the sense of neutrality'.[16] The rise of architects and practices with signature forms and material palette at their disposal – ready to be deployed in any corner of the globe at the first available opportunity – unfortunately removes that potential for optimising the perceptual contribution of materials.

Although 'the high ground of modern architecture was commanded by a dematerialized vision of space and time as the basis for the international style',[17] as Weston contends, the oeuvres of Gunnar Asplund and Wright, beside the post-Second World War work of Neutra, Scarpa, Aalto and Kahn, and certain works of Le Corbusier, confirm the continued engagement with the inescapable role of materiality in place-making. While the use of typical, entirely local materials in these works would have resulted in 'buildings of intrusive banality',[18] the exclusive use of 'modern', universal materials would have equally eliminated the sense of place. Expressing the sense of place through the use of local materials could transcend the banal superficiality resulting from their overly familiar use, as Leatherbarrow reminds us. A fragment–whole relationship is strongly present in Casa dei Filippini, where Borromini wanted to render visible through its materiality the iconic mother–child relationship between the Casa and its mother, the Santa.[19] This was done by introducing travertine from the Santa into the body of

the Casa. The dominant use of brick at the Casa suggests modesty with respect to the rich maturity of the travertine at the Santa.

Wearing certain tones or colours of a locale could provide architecture with the opportunity to present the past in a new light. This would not necessarily mean a detachment from the contemporary; rather, it could be seen as an attempt at anchoring the new into the history of a place. Jean Philippe Lenclos analyses the colours he finds that constitute a colour palette of the vicinity for his intervention in that environment.[20] Material and colour theory for the city, he contends, 'has to be seen in this greater context and used, where that is possible, for decorating the city by creating harmony where none may exist'.[21] The accord between art and earthwork is vividly apparent, as Leatherbarrow suggests, 'when colour is used in construction finishing, for hues made out of local pigments will always result in relationships of harmony'.[22] Charles Correa's use of sandstone cladding at both the Jawahar Kala Kendra and the British Council Headquarters does indicate a desire to conform to local architectural and material precedents in Jaipur and Delhi (Figure 6.2). Conforming to place identity through materials is not necessarily an obstacle for architectonic and structural expressions either; responding to both the materials and tones found in the locale, Michael Rotondi combined inventive architectural form with contextuality at the Architecture and Art Building at Prairie View A&M University (Figure 6.3), highlighting the versatility of the brick as a structural material. As Amelar points out, Rotondi's retrieval of original and authentic structural methods makes the brickwork become extraordinary within a contemporary context: 'Using old-fashioned, wire-cut clay bricks, instead of the more artificial-looking versions that clad the surrounding buildings, RoTo inventively explored corbelling, displaying a jubilant range of possibilities.'[23]

Sensitivity to place morphology requires considering its *genius loci*. The later essays of Wright addressed methods

136   Enis Aldallal | Site and Composition: Design strategies
Husam AlWaer and | in architecture and urbanism
Soumyen Bandyopadhyay |

Figure 6.2 Charles Correa. British Council Headquarters, Delhi: front facade detail showing red sandstone cladding.

that envisioned the employment of modern materials at different places, suggesting that their widened significance lay in expanded visionary insights into how those materials could be treated and transformed through new artistic methods.[24] In fact, his meditation on place and transformation of both new and old materials had inspired a second generation of modern architects like Richard Neutra,

who attempted to retrieve the tactile delights of materials that early modernism had so vehemently shunned. Carlo Scarpa was also among those who attempted novel poetic compositional strategies using modern materials like concrete, steel and glass in contexts where building with brick and stone had had its traditional place. Through sensitive contextual derivation, Wright allowed inflection to occur that retained the whole but avoided literal imitation. At Taliesin West he had collected rocks from the immediate vicinity of the site, setting those in concrete, technologically transforming the material, 'tattooing' the building with the surrounding topography in the process. Several stone walls and a central stone fireplace, combined with careful placement of local rocks and boulders, form a close link with

Figure 6.3 RoTo Architects. Architecture and Art Building, A&M University, Prairie View, Texas: undulated brick masonry wall (after photograph in www.rotoark.com/projects/education-cultural-civic/prairie-view-university, accessed 11 April 2015).

the surrounding arid landscape at Neutra's Kaufmann House in Palm Springs, California. The coexistence of the dressed stone quarried at a mine in Utah, and the natural form of the local rocks, created a simultaneous ambiguity and extension of the local, blurring the boundary between where the local ended and the regional/global began. At the Guggenheim Museum, New York, Wright expressed the fluid topography of city life and its non-stop movement into concrete ramps addressing 'the new aesthetic of continuity' of concrete sidewalks.[25] A similar attempt at blurring distinctions between the site and the movement network of the immediate context is present in Zaha Hadid's Contemporary Arts Centre in Cincinnati, where the poured-in-place boundary is morphed to form both the museum's entry hall floor and the walkway on the outside of the museum, drawing in the urban carpet of the surroundings (Figure 6.4). At the CaixaForum in Madrid Herzog & de Meuron's strategy was to use acid-oxidised metal panels to bring a rich appearance of colour and texture to the extension to respond to the brick of the original power station (Figure 6.5).[26] Through its colour, texture and geometry, the building has succeeded in blending in with its surroundings without losing its contemporary identity.

Richard Weston had argued for a more anthropologically attuned understanding of the nature of material employment when he had concluded:

> The interaction of materials and place confirms that any attempt to understand the 'nature', as opposed to quantifiable properties, of materials independently of their use in a specific location is misleading. Ignoring this relationship may suit the aspirations of those [whose] reasoning is grounded in ideology, not the science of materials – whose qualities and meanings in architecture are inescapably place specific and time-bound.[27]

The importance of such selection criteria cannot be overstated in today's divergent practices and trends where,

Figure 6.4 Zaha Hadid. Contemporary Arts Centre, Cincinnati, Ohio: material continuity between the sidewalk and the lobby.

given the multiplicity of materials that are at the ready disposal of the architect, the 'temptation to use them cosmetically is strong'.[28] While there is nothing inherently problematic about the use of materials as cladding, the validity of such use needs to be ascertained against human engagement and inhabitation that is temporally and geographically specific. The above discussion has covered the 'locale' where the site sits and interacts with its immediate surroundings. The following discussion addresses the 'regional' scale by examining how the regional or the global can affect the architectural language of the local.

Regional materials or the influence of ultimate context

In the Casa, Borromini dealt with brick in a different way from others who built in that locale. His use of brick

138   Enis Aldallal | Site and Composition: Design strategies
Husam AlWaer and | in architecture and urbanism
Soumyen Bandyopadhyay |

Figure 6.5 Herzog & de Meuron. CaixaForum Building, Madrid: juxtaposition of old brick facade and acid-oxidised metal clad extension.

addressed an interrelationship between the Santa and her daughter, the Casa, as fragments of a larger whole. Such dialogue was achieved by Borromini taking into account

materials of the locale and the wider region. The regional materiality that emerges, therefore, acknowledges the need for material selection based on both the local and the wider context. While the latter could be understood geographically at the scale of a city, a country or even an entire continent, it does not necessarily preclude the possibility of the use of a single material that is available in abundance within a region. This is because the true 'topographical possibilities'[29] of a material could be expanded through the intervention of technique, i.e. technological transformation could potentially give shape to the regionality of a material.

Manifestations of this kind coincide with the idea of articulating the wider topography of a place rather than restoring regional identity solely through narrow instrumental responses.[30] Yet, responding to the characteristics of the encompassing terrain could provide a way into this complex phenomenon. The latter is the case at Wright's Taliesin West and Neutra's Kaufmann House, where the material attributes of the immediate terrain were seen as a means of accessing the immaterial – the one that was difficult to fathom. This also appears to be the case in the works of Jørn Utzon, the oeuvre of Geoffrey Bawa,[31] and as Leatherbarrow so aptly demonstrates, in those of Aris Konstantinidis at Mykonos and Anavyssos in Greece.[32] What characterises these architectures is the use of regional materials – like stone and marble – quarried in or near their sites. The materials are transformed through technological applications setting them perceptually apart from the ones that originally existed on site, or by carefully interrupting the topographic continuity of the locale through contrasting material use.[33] Therefore, 'material expression can be understood only in a larger context embracing the place',[34] where successful material deployment is again capable of constructing a liminal, regional materiality, crystallising the tension between the local and the wider topographic contexts into moments of accentuated dialogue celebrating place identity.

An example of this accentuated dialogue could be found in Siza's Galician Centre for Contemporary Art (Figure 6.6), of which we have already examined the spatial reciprocity

between the inside and the outside – between site and place (see Chapter 5). Here, to resist the loss of place identity, he sought to make references simultaneously to the immediate and the ultimate context. Although initially contemplating an entirely contrasting appearance in concrete, Siza eventually sought to hide his contemporary building, making it subservient to the medieval monastery that provides its context.[35] His material references are twofold; the locale of the museum embraces a number of classic buildings built in granite – one of them being the convent of Santo Domingo de Bonaval. However, it is the abstracted manner in which the museum employs the granite on the outside – transformed through technology into a thin, contemporary veneer – that sets it apart from the demanding, conservative existence of the Convent, simultaneously alluding to the regional – Galician – employment of the same material. Significantly, as Moneo points out, a single material – granite – 'becomes the protagonist'.[36] In contrast, on the inside, Siza has used rendered wall surfaces painted white, referring to a local finish – the white stucco – that covers the majority of the city of Santiago de Compostela. In employing the white stucco on the inside and the granite on the outside, Siza's approach to this project was as much practical as it was theoretical. Siza commented on the granite: 'I … thought that there was a case to be made for introducing a non-local material to an exceptional building in an exceptional part of the city. We should not be afraid of that.'[37] To him, using a material with wider regional resonance against an interiorised local materiality was a way of opening up a channel of communication with the immediate context, as well as for establishing a dialogue with history.

History, collective memory and regionalism returned to the site as driving forces in the process of materialising the museum and enabled this highly contemporary intervention to address its place identity. Here, spatial play and materiality have combined to reconcile the opposites between new/old, local/regional and inside/outside. The result of this compromise is what Kenneth Frampton

140   Enis Aldallal | Site and Composition: Design strategies
Husam AlWaer and | in architecture and urbanism
Soumyen Bandyopadhyay |

describes as an architecture that 'depends … as much upon the materials and the general tone of the ambient light as it does upon the specific nature of the space'.[38] A similar attempt to restore the historical memory was undertaken by Peter Eisenman through the incomplete, deconstructed brick towers at the Wexner Centre, which recalled the once-present Armory towers (Figure 6.7).

The early work of the Indian architect Charles Correa suggests a subtle reworking of a largely International vocabulary and material palette to reflect emergent regional and local dimensions. The Gandhi Memorial Museum in Ahmedabad (1963; Figure 6.8), where the immediate context was provided by the vernacular structures of Mahatma Gandhi's Sabarmati Ashram, was designed following a 6 m × 6 m grid. The raised plinth,

Figure 6.6 Alvaro Siza. Galician Centre for Contemporary Art, Santiago de Compostela.

Figure 6.7 Peter Eisenman. The Wexner Centre for the Visual Arts, Ohio State University, Columbus, Ohio: the fragmented presence of brick masonry.

compositional aspects and formal iconography make direct references to the Memorial Museum's immediate context but also to their roots in the International style. The brick piers and horizontal concrete elements, together, represent both the local and the global. Kahn's Indian Institute of Management – but also Le Corbusier's Sarabhai House – now indelible icons of Ahmedabad's architectural heritage, had just been completed. Correa drew on this recently developed 'local' palette, which by proxy had introduced into Ahmedabad a post-Independence regional (Indian) interpretation of the International material palette. On the

outside, the brick piers appear to prop up the horizontal concrete plate, a condition reversed on the inside, especially around the courtyard, where the brick piers appear to be floating, held between the strong horizontal concrete members: the continuous floor plate and the grid of the roof beams.[39] This material-tectonic reciprocity closely corresponds with the spatial reciprocity between the inside and the outside at Le Corbusier's Mill Owners' Association (see Chapter 5) – both products of highly porous or, in the case of Correa, even non-existent facades. The fragility of the surrounding Ashram hutment, where Gandhi lived for

142   Enis Aldallal | Site and Composition: Design strategies
Husam AlWaer and | in architecture and urbanism
Soumyen Bandyopadhyay |

Figure 6.8 Charles Correa. The Gandhi Memorial Museum, Ahmedabad: brick piers, rural iconography and the raised plinth create a 'horizontal' monument to Mahatma Gandhi.

12 years, was interpreted as lightweight infill panels with open louvered windows standing on the edge of stone-clad floor planes (Figure 6.9), and the more directly derived clay tile-clad pyramidal roof. They also remind us of the decorated timber infill panels found on facades of houses in Old Ahmedabad. Yet, employed carefully to capture both the spirit of Mahatma Gandhi's Ashram, as well as to respond to the anthropological demands placed on the new building, the horizontality, combined with a taut and ingenious material deployment, simultaneously produced the memorial and the universal receptacle of the museum. Materiality thus fused context with use, leaving one to

wonder whether this material deployment introduced a liminal – that is, regional – materiality, suspended between the local and the universal. The term 'regional', here, acquires a meta-geographical connotation. This is perhaps what Leatherbarrow means by suggesting that all materials are regional; that is, to transcend an instrumental application all successful material employment would necessarily need to consider their 'regionality' to uphold a deeper understanding of the more immediate context.

Materiality could also aid the crystallisation of contexts where none readily exists. While this might sound unusual,

Figure 6.9 Gandhi Memorial Museum: infill panels, view from one of the gallery interiors and exterior view.

consideration of two of Correa's other early works – both temporary structures built for trade fairs – would make this point clearer. The Handloom Pavilion (1958, Figure 6.10) at the International Fair and the Hindustan Lever Pavilion (1961, Figure 6.11) at the Industrial Fair, both in Delhi, were designed as temporary exhibition venues for an independent India searching for its identity. In both, consideration of a much wider context provides material manifestation. At the Handloom Pavilion, a space enclosed by the rendered brick and mud walls was covered by a number of 'inverted' umbrella-like canopies constructed of timber frames and covered in polychromatic handloom fabric. Albeit transformed through technological reshaping, together they provide material manifestation to the quintessential setting of handloom production – a

somewhat distanced, yet pervasive, rural environment. At the Hindustan Lever Pavilion – where Correa continued to explore the potential of the *promenade architectural* – the elaborately folded sprayed reinforced concrete enclosure assumes the form of a giant crumpled packing crate – complete with the broken legends of this corporate institution boldly stencilled over, alluding to both the highly international commercial enterprise in question, as well as the temporary nature of the exhibition venue. Through its rustic incompleteness, the material employed draws in and questions presumptions regarding the sophisticated nature of multinational establishments and a linear relationship between material employment and transience in architecture.

The play of mediating boundaries

> As an intermediary object the work of architecture does not describe the world, rather it unifies some of its aspects in a new meaningful whole.
>
> Norberg-Schulz[40]

The above discussion highlights the mediating role of materiality; it is a condition that stands in between and makes manifest the interface between the inside and the outside, and between the local and the global. At the Casa de Piedra (Stone House) in Tavole, Italy (1985; Figure 6.12), Herzog & de Meuron employ a method of selective revelation and extension of the concrete frame to establish continuity with the mountainous surroundings. Designed as a stone cuboid with carefully composed facades consisting of a limited number of openings, the architects have sought to hide the concrete corner columns by encasing them in stone. The resulting appearance of completeness of the stone volume allows a geological continuity between the dry stone masonry of the building and its surroundings. This continuity is further strengthened by the revelation of columns at or near the centre of the facades, providing the edges with a sense of floating, boundless extension.

144 Enis Aldallal | Site and Composition: Design strategies
Husam AlWaer and | in architecture and urbanism
Soumyen Bandyopadhyay |

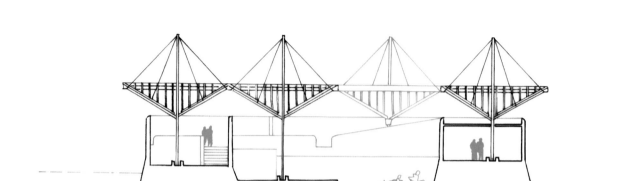

Figure 6.10 Charles Correa. Handloom Pavilion, Delhi (1958): section showing mud walls and fabric 'parasols' (after Khan, H., 1987 *Charles Correa*).

Figure 6.11 Charles Correa. Hindustan Lever Pavilion, Delhi (1961): formal study (after Khan, H., 1987 *Charles Correa*).

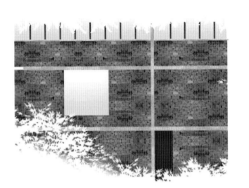

Figure 6.12 Herzog & de Meuron. Casa de Piedra (Stone House),
Tavole: facade study (after Leatherbarrow, D., 2004 *Topographical
Stories*).

Although the building appears as a closed box on site,
suggesting minimal relationship with the inside and thus
with inhabitation, the abstract concrete frame, which
orchestrates the few openings, extends beyond to suggest
extension of the inhabited interior.

Sites and buildings stand between local and global
contexts and topographies, helping to accentuate their
dialogue through the building's materiality. In Correa's
exhibition pavilions, highly defined boundaries existed
between the inside and the outside, as the pavilions
sought to address a wider context in the absence of an
immediate one. Physically and anthropologically defined
interiors were thereby carved out from wider cultural
topographies of rurban India, on the one end, and the
corporate world of global multinationals, on the other. At
the Hindustan Lever Pavilion the defined boundaries spoke
of a captured moment where the interior space seemed
to have been locked in an existential struggle with the
pulverising forces of the corporate, yet managing to fight
back somehow, resulting in a contorted concrete interface.
The entrance and exit shafts, the connecting *promenade
architectural* and the cannon-like top-lights employed
to set up air convection currents,[41] which provided the

means of sustenance for the interior, also introduced a
degree of porosity into the otherwise impervious shell
of the pavilion. The devices introduced permeability of
people, air and light, and brought the materiality of the
outside in and inside out. The *promenade* also breached
the square enclosure at the decidedly more serene and
stable – yet equally defined – Handloom Pavilion. The
polychrome fabric canopies – much like sails – responded
to the changes in the external environment, affecting light
conditions and air movement inside. While the pavilions
followed Heidegger's observation that, 'people identify
places for themselves by lassoing "boundaries" around
them in their minds',[42] these boundaries, however, were
never fully defined. The architectural fragments and their
materiality, sitting between an 'interior' and an 'exterior',
introduced, and were introduced by, people and the
environment passing over and through them.

At the Pritzker Family Children's Zoo in Lincoln Park Zoo,
Chicago (2005; Figure 6.13) by EHDD, the transmittance of
materials through boundaries or in-between zones is what
helps perform mediation between outside and inside. Its
materialisation in concrete and glass curtain walling and the
crisp geometry of the facade are fronted by a tension cable
grid supporting an 'ivy wall'. While the bold orthogonal
geometry of the building extends out to the grid, the
growing ivy markedly softens its harshness, integrating
with and extending inwards the natural exuberance of
the zoo precinct. Externally, the glass curtain wall helps
'thicken' the greenery through reflection. From the inside,
the ivy frame – or in fact, the combined materiality of the
in-between – modifies the climatic conditions on its way in,
being itself modified by the varying climatic impact over the
seasons. Visually, a visitor perceives the building to extend
beyond the glass panels to the ivy screen, which now frames
the outside more acutely as one peers through it; a kind of
active porosity has thus been achieved.

Venturi conceived material mediation among spaces as the
'graduated series of things in things or enclosures within

146 Enis Aldallal | Site and Composition: Design strategies
Husam AlWaer and | in architecture and urbanism
Soumyen Bandyopadhyay |

Figure 6.13 EHDD. Pritzker Family Children's Zoo, Lincoln Park Zoo, Chicago, Illinois: facade detail with the 'ivy wall'.

enclosures',[43] a condition Leatherbarrow also elaborated through the relationship of material 'in-ness' between Borromini's *Casa* and the *Santa*. The intermediary role of the architectural object is highlighted where the materiality of one is brought within the other, manifesting a higher level of connectedness through a distended understanding of their boundaries. The prominent marks made on the fireplace of Aris Konstantinidis' Weekend House at Anavyssos, Greece (1962), draw the surrounding terrain into the house.[44] Aided by the porosity of the external

fabric, the implicit continuity between topography and the unpolished concrete panel on the fireplace was achieved through a cryptic, 'barely figurative' – yet economic – notation crystallising the topographic attributes of the surroundings.[45]

Porosity amounts to a near dismantling of the facade at the Gandhi Memorial Museum as the surrounding context – or perhaps we should say, contexts – invade the building's 'interior' (Figure 6.14). The rhythm and regularity of the brick piers and the overhead grid of concrete beams draw on an optimism expressed not that long ago through an identical austere modern vocabulary by Le Corbusier and Kahn. This quintessentially post-Independence Ahmedabad interior is infiltrated by the sun but also the gentle breeze from the river Sabarmati, bringing it ever so close to the exterior. Playing out the rhythmic dance of light and shadows on the brick piers, and the occasional reflection of ripples from the central water court, the building could be seen as the crystallisation of the relationship that had existed between water, land and human habitation, whose main aim was to provide shade within this relatively inhospitable terrain. Horizontality is enhanced by the darkness of the timber-clad ceilings of the pyramidal roofs and the dark stone floor, focusing the visitors' mind on the sun-drenched, carefully composed focal courtyards, the strong horizontal character of the louvered infill panels, and the benches to rest on, which emerge as topographic notations from the floor. The benches further highlight the dominant horizontality of the building by establishing datum points as moments of repose, giving prominence to the streets and passages that now emerge from the extensive and continuous floor plane, carved out through the placement of disaggregated spaces for the display of artefacts. Correa has written extensively about both the rural origins and the benefits of employing the disaggregated architectural form, which results in a 'series of separate but interdependent volumes'.[46] Scale, horizontality, streetscape and the tiled pyramidal roofs add to the rural character of the Museum. The heavy brick piers and staggered stone paving indicate a strong influence of the Sarabhai House, yet the floor along with the infill panels and the sloped roof speak of the persistent presence of the disaggregated rural dwellings of Gandhi's Sabarmati Ashram as originally established. Suspended among Ahmedabad's emerging architectural modernity, a strong expression of the rural, and a sensitive appreciation of the natural setting, the museum's true interior – the memorabilia repositories – recedes into its disaggregated cells – like Gandhi's Ashram, isolated, yet deeply interconnected through a unified mission. Closely

guarding the relics of Gandhi's life, the museum expresses the Gandhian world in microcosm.

Conclusion: camouflage

Materiality is the projective relationship between drawing and building; the appropriate use of building materials manifesting an architectural form and appearance could better align a building with its site and the anthropological demands, through inhabitation and perception. By focusing on materiality of a building located on a site, the intermediary role of the latter in place-making and its transformation is highlighted. It also relies on the fact that the architectural character of site lies in the character and qualities of its different surfaces, which in turn have a direct relationship to the embracing place.[47] Following Frampton and Leatherbarrow, this chapter has identified two extensions of the topographic horizon; the *immediate context* – the locale – and the *ultimate context* – the regional, initially considered as offering distinctive material opportunities in order to address place identity. However, the discussion has soon highlighted the problematic nature of an instrumental consideration of local context, suggesting instead the need for a meta-geographical – *regional* – understanding of materiality that transcends the abovementioned contextual distinctions and embraces its anthropological dimension.

The interplay between local and ultimate contexts makes manifest the distinguishing boundary between inside and outside through which material negotiations take place. The characteristics of such boundaries were explored, moving from highly defined ones where spatiality and materiality coincided in establishing distinctions, to more fluid and distended relationships where materiality was transported and transmitted across spatial boundaries to articulate the overlapping and latent contextual terrains. The resultant spatiality and materiality acquire the characteristics of a liminal field, where the architectural object is in a perpetual state of becoming, highlighting the mediatory and

148   Enis Aldallal | Site and Composition: Design strategies
       Husam AlWaer and | in architecture and urbanism
Soumyen Bandyopadhyay |

Figure 6.14 Gandhi Memorial Museum: porosity of the interior.

perpetually re-constructed nature of sites. Engaging the perceptual qualities of materials to the fullest – their colours, textures and other actual material attributes, but also their extensions in perceived densities, roughness, lightness or darkness – allows the designer the flexibility to articulate complex contextual overlaps.

This chapter has sought to approach the site as a fragment that dissolves into the canvas of its context, emerging from its place history, its collective memories and experiences, and enriching it on its return. This implies a peculiar kind of role any site necessarily needs to perform: a performance

in which material transmission and reciprocity across contexts, and between context and inhabitation, plays a critical role. Through a number of architectural examples this chapter has examined divergent methods of interaction that sought to keep place and site interdependent, in which the architectural project played a facilitating and revelatory role. Here, the new anthropological demands – the requirements and demands placed on a site through new inhabitation and their implications – acted as catalysts for making, re-making and enriching the place. While Correa's exhibition pavilions had to invent site and place within what could be termed a *non-place* (the fairground),

the Gandhi Memorial Museum was essentially a reworking
of many contexts: local, the wider regional and the fast-
emerging context of Indian architectural modernity. At
Casa de Piedra, Herzog & de Meuron cautiously announced
new inhabitation through the extension of the concrete
frame beyond the stone cuboids. Pushing the boundaries of
materialisation further towards the idea of reciprocity, not
only between site and context but also between site and its
interiors, has transported the concrete urban carpet of the
Galician Centre for Contemporary Art into a poetic dialogue
between the entrance lobby and the monochromic
sidewalks of the city.

150   Enis Aldallal | Site and Composition: Design strategies
         Husam AlWaer and | in architecture and urbanism
    Soumyen Bandyopadhyay |

Notes

1 Leatherbarrow, D., *Uncommon Ground*, Cambridge, MA: MIT Press, 2002, p. 233.

2 Leatherbarrow, D., *Architecture Oriented Otherwise*, New York: Princeton Architectural Press, 2009, p. 243.

3 Ibid.

4 Zevi, B., *Architecture as Space*, New York: Horizon Press, 1957, p. 29.

5 Dovey, K., *Framing Places: Mediating Power in Built Environment*, New York: Routledge, 1999, p. 50.

6 Sharr, A., *Thinkers for Architects: Heidegger for Architects*, New York: Routledge, 2007, p. 63.

7 Pallasmaa, J., 'An Architecture of the Seven Senses', in Holl, S., Pallasmaa, J. & Pérez Gómez, A., *A+U: Questions of Perception: Phenomenology of Architecture*, San Francisco, CA: William Stout Publishers, 2007, p. 30.

8 Norberg-Schulz, C. (Nasso, C. & Parini, S., eds; Shugaar, A., trans.), *Architecture: Presence, Language and Place*, Milan: Skira, 2000, p. 223.

9 Blundell-Jones, P., *Gunnar Asplund*, London: Phaidon Press, 2006, p. 229.

10 Yoshida, N. & Zumthor, P., *A+U: Peter Zumthor*, Tokyo: A+U Publishing, February 1998 extra edition, p. 16.

11 Abercrombie, S., *Architecture as Art*, New York: Harper & Row, 1984, p. 96.

12 Norberg-Schulz, op. cit., p. 159.

13 An essay first published in *Perspecta* in 1983, in which Frampton's contribution was to suggest a compromise between the extremes of Enlightenment idealism and New Historic materialism. Frampton, K., 'Prospects for a Critical *Regionalism*', *Perspecta* 20, 1983, pp. 147–162.

14 Frampton, K., 'Towards a Critical Regionalism: Six Points for an Architecture of Resistance', in Jencks, C. & Kropf, K. (eds) *Theories and Manifestoes of Contemporary Architecture* (second edition), London: Wiley Academy, 2006, p. 97.

15 Leatherbarrow, D., *The Roots of Architectural Invention: Site, Enclosure, Materials*, Cambridge: Cambridge University Press, 1993, p. 146.

16 Rykwert, J., *The Necessity of Artifice*, London: Academy Editions, 1982, p. 59.

17 Weston, R., *Materials, Form and Architecture*, London: Laurence King, 2003, p. 100.

18 Ibid., p. 109.

19 Leatherbarrow, *Roots of Architectural Invention*, p. 173.

20 Moughtin, C., Oc, T. & Tiesdell, S., 'Colour in the City', in Trasi, N. (ed.), *Interdisciplinary Architecture*, London: Wiley Academy, 2001, p. 70.

21 Ibid., p. 68.

22 Leatherbarrow, *Uncommon Ground*, p. 190.

23 Amelar, S., 'Architecture and Art Building', *Architectural Record*, 1/2006, 2006, p. 105.

24 Hearn, M., *Ideas that Shaped Buildings*, Cambridge, MA: MIT Press, 2003, p. 264.

25 Weston, op. cit., p. 92.

26 'CaixaForum, Madrid', *Architecture + Urbanism (A+U)* 5/2008, 2008, p. 25.

27 Weston, op. cit., p. 114.

28 Smith, P., *Architecture and the Principle of Harmony*, London, RIBA, 1987, p. 135.

29 Leatherbarrow, *Roots of Architectural Invention*, p. 146.

30 Leatherbarrow, *Uncommon Ground*, p. 213; also, Leatherbarrow, *Roots of Architectural Invention*, p. ix.

31 Taylor, B., *Geoffrey Bawa*, New York: Concept Media, 1986, p. 9.

32 Leatherbarrow, *Uncommon Ground*, p. 189.

33 Ibid., p. 191.

34 Weston, op. cit., p. 43.

35 Frampton, K. & Siza, A., *Alvaro Siza: The Complete Works*, London: Phaidon, 2000, p. 336.

36 Moneo, R., *Theoretical Anxiety and Design Strategies in the Work of Eight Contemporary Architects*, Cambridge, MA: MIT Press, 2004, p. 247.

37 Frampton, K. (2000) 'Architecture as Critical Transformation: The Work of Álvaro Siza', in Frampton, K. & Siza, A., *Alvaro Siza: Complete Works*, London: Phaidon, p. 49.

38 Ibid., p. 46.

39 Substantial brickwork inclines also 'hold' the rectangular
   wedged-in window element at Correa's Ramkrishna House in
   Ahmedabad, a building with strong echoes of the Sarabhai
   House. In fact, both of Correa's buildings indicate the capped
   horizontality produced through the use of clearly articulated
   concrete members. See, Khan, H., *Charles Correa: Architect in India*,
   Singapore and London: Mimar/Butterworth, 1987, pp. 32–35.

40 Norberg-Schulz, C., *Intentions in Architecture*, Cambridge, MA:
   MIT Press, 1968, p. 179.

41 Khan, op. cit., p. 30.

42 Sharr, op. cit., p. 62.

43 Venturi, R., *Complexity and Contradiction in Architecture*, New
   York: Museum of Modern Art, 1977, p. 74.

44 Leatherbarrow, *Uncommon Ground*, p. 217.

45 Ibid., p. 213.

46 Correa, C., 'Transfer and Transformations', in Khan, H., *Charles
   Correa: Architect in India*, Singapore and London: Mimar/
   Butterworth, 1987, p. 166.

47 Leatherbarrow, *Roots of Architectural Invention*, p. 215.

7 Conclusion

154   Enis Aldallal | Site and Composition: Design strategies
Husam AlWaer and | in architecture and urbanism
Soumyen Bandyopadhyay |

The book is concerned with the need for a renewed understanding of the site in the twenty-first century and the establishment of a critical position *vis-à-vis* the continued tendency to regard it as a fragment severed from its wider context. This tendency, fuelled by the demands of globalisation, effectively extends one of the most problematic aspects of the modernist treatment of the site as a given, isolatable entity, itself emanating from modernism's obsession with the idea of the 'fragment'. The problem with this decoupling has been the denial of the effect of the encompassing forces that inevitably act on a site, as well as the failure to read the site's extended impact following design action. The result is the impoverished architectural, landscape and urban design actions, which emerge as a series of unconnected contiguities, unresolved in their relationship. The site's perceived isolation offers the architect the dubious opportunity to produce novel forms that vie with each other for attention.

The reduction of the site into simple information sets has no doubt helped designers – often operating remotely in today's globalised world of architectural practice – to produce buildings with relative ease and within demanding time constraints. However, this has also reduced the immense complexity of the site into little more than simplified geometries – mainly the result of abstracted plot boundaries indicating legal limits. Site specificity is largely ignored and an overly simplified instrumentality has prevailed in dealing with site and design. As discussed in our Introduction, even as we have to treat sites increasingly as assemblages of orthogonal projections, such abstraction need not necessarily prevent us from considering deeper, often latent and less obvious information and knowledge about the site. Instrumentality and abstract codification *per se*, we argue, are not the problem, and as Alberti's survey of Rome demonstrates, are even critical to our understanding of orders of things. It is the counter-creative and anti-anthropological manner in which we have increasingly treated such material that has caused the crisis.

A *crisis*, however, is also an opportunity for introspection never to be wasted. Creativity and research have always existed at the heart of architectural education and practice – an advantageous condition the discipline should strive to maintain. Research has been central to architectural design; in fact, one could argue that the architectural design discipline has largely – and uniquely – remained research-led. The essentially creative nature of research (and by extension, of design inquiry) is acknowledged in Kant's recognition of the close relationship between creativity and imagination and his suggestion of the central role of the latter in furthering understanding underpinning cognition. The reciprocity between imagination and the ever-expanding and consolidating horizons of understanding of both the human and the natural condition would therefore question the relevance of the notion of *creation ex nihilo* – i.e. the belief that true creative ideas emerge out of nowhere, more often the force behind the drive for novelty. Equally problematic is the belief in creativity as a patchwork of ideas and methods indiscriminately drawn from other disciplines, since both approaches are products of a weak – incomplete – understanding of the condition. Creative imagination is thus only bounded by this ever-expanding horizon of understanding in which both extant and emergent knowledge co-mingle. This provides a renewed opportunity for establishing the fragment's lost connections with the whole.

Artificially privileging the present-day knowledge and information over historical understanding and *vice versa* have resulted in the plethora of instruments – many of which are, in fact, borrowed from other disciplines – that have merely allowed the multitudinous expansion in architecture's productive capacity. Both, however, have, at various points in history, put emphasis on the *entirely* formal qualities of the built object – the architectural figure. Treated thus, architecture's performative qualities and its essentially anthropological nature – which abstraction had proposed to capture in the first place – have fallen by the wayside; what have remained as the only possible avenues

156   Enis Aldallal | Site and Composition: Design strategies
Husam AlWaer and | in architecture and urbanism
Soumyen Bandyopadhyay |

of mounting a critique of such architectural products are the narrow – and by now contested – understandings of aesthetic codes and functionality. The conveniently reduced scope of the condition under scrutiny has resulted in the impoverishment of architecture and the accumulation of detritus. Our existence increasingly is one of a foreigner imprisoned in the socio-cultural debris of our own creation.

In architectural design the problem also lies in the simple binary oppositions we have conveniently established for ourselves – often in the name of professional practice – between past and present, function and meaning, rational and irrational, object and performance, instrumental and existential, between architecture and non-architecture, and so on. Such oppositions emanated from the positional and disciplinary fissures that occurred during the early Enlightenment, only to be re-emphasised through the emergence of the professional architectural training in the late eighteenth and nineteenth centuries. The fissure, paradoxically, lies in the development of instrumental thinking in mideighteenth century theorising, especially through Durand's work at the École Polytechnique, which also indicated the beginnings of overt technological intentionality. As a result, technology emerged as a utopia and a universal mentality configuring the modern world, extracting its potency from the human capacity to abstract. This relatively recent phenomenon has contributed to a certain kind of determinism and a calculated appropriation of reality. Such intensely abstracted abstractions – of which Mondrian's paintings are good examples – have removed the primordial experiences that humans have shared since time immemorial as embodied, spatially oriented individuals, managing only to achieve universality at the expense of meaning. As this book argues, it is vital that we optimise the potential of the existential *through* the instrumental codifications of relationships between architecture and its widest context.

Confronting these tendencies, this book has argued for revisiting the instruments of both siting and composition

in architecture to explore their true potential in achieving connections between site and context. It focused on architects of wide-ranging persuasions of the twentieth century – for example, Peter Eisenman, Le Corbusier, Frank Lloyd Wright, Alvaro Siza, Herzog & de Meuron and Charles Correa – whose works defy categorisation under simple binary oppositions. Through the various examples studied here, we suggest that the instrumental means have the potential for enhanced analogical and scalar relationships capable of achieving poetic outcomes. The dominant modernist tendency to regard the world around us as a fragmented phenomenon, which replaced the world of pre-modern certainty, has been found inadequate in the postmodern era of globalisation, and amidst a renewed interest in achieving wholeness. Chapter 1 also attempted to map the historical trajectory of the fragment. Contrary to a commonly held notion that fragmentation results in severed and emancipated unconnected entities with no histories, we have favoured the view that fragments within a culture are continually both created and received – inflecting the fragment, as well as reshaping the context. They are historical in the sense that they contain characteristics and values resident in the whole. We have focused mainly – although not exclusively – on the potential of the planimetric treatment of the site and its surroundings.

Sites are essentially artificially constructed phenomena, be it through the establishment of abstract property boundaries or the inevitable selective consideration of site conditions. Perhaps surprisingly, both Le Corbusier and Peter Eisenman share an interest in the creative and imaginative potential of sites as artificial constructions: Le Corbusier's post-Second World War projects in India and Eisenman's *artificial excavation* projects of the 1980s bear testimony to this exploration. Chapter 2 extended the study of the fragmentary nature of the site by considering Le Corbusier's construction of site at the Capitol in Chandigarh, India. There we argued that he regarded the constructed site as a collection or an 'archipelago' of fragments, the irreducible, resilient remains of a culture – its essence, as it were – that stood composed on an artificial *tabula rasa* formed by the forcible removal and burial of the once-encumbering detritus. Distinct from breaking up, the process of fragment formation – fragmentation – here, was to do with reducing it to the irreducible – the essence. Extending Vidler's assertion, we argue that the fragments at Chandigarh and Ahmedabad suggest the presence of not only narratives, but meta-narratives: they are both historical and yet ahistorical – primordial, *positive* entities capable of achieving renewed wholeness. This denuded primordial armature made possible the exploration of issues of social justice that seems to have been at the heart of Le Corbusier's Indian projects exploring post-Independence concerns surrounding equality and universal access to resources. Abstracted tapestry of assembled fragments re-applied as garbing produced a fragile, theatrical setting for anthropological actions, which enabled Chandigarh to embrace the 'other' – abstract and non-contiguous but nevertheless critical – sites of culture, while maintaining, at the same time, certain problematic relationships with its immediate physical surroundings.

Considering further the nature of the 'positive' fragment and the role it could potentially play in the sustenance of the built environment, in Chapter 3 we directed our attention to the site's relationship with its immediate surroundings. The importance of edge conditions as the key facilitator for achieving interrelationship between sites, as well as between architectural objects, was highlighted. Peter Eisenman's design for the Wexner Centre, we argued, fulfils this role as a positive fragment mediating between the Ohio State University campus and the city of Columbus. This was undertaken on plan through a series of mainly instrumental moves with far-reaching effect. However, like Le Corbusier's Chandigarh, it was also concerned with wider themes of American history and the politics of cultural memory of the preceding centuries. The abstract grid is employed here for site construction into which reconstituted fragments from the past are reinserted to provide legibility and continuity. It establishes a significant interplay between

the modernist grid and postmodern fragments carrying historical resonance. In both Le Corbusier's Atelier Ozenfant in Paris and Eisenman's Aronoff Centre at the University of Cincinnati we find a developed sectional understanding of both sites and evolving buildings as positive fragments. Instrumental manipulations, we demonstrate, remain at the heart of Eisenman's commitment to integrating site characteristics and the existing buildings, as well as his aim to embrace the less material but crucial spirit of the institution. In attempting to connect, territorial edges need to be imaginatively reactivated to establish novel conjunctions, creating a new wholeness through considered and creative instrumental manipulation.

In Chapter 4 we considered more carefully the role of planimetric drawing and composition in achieving meaningful relationships between building and site and between site and its wider context. The role of drawn studies and developmental orthogonal projections in providing the autonomous fora for the convergence of the site and design intentions through interpretation and crafting is highlighted. Projective drawings are, as examples as diverse as Gothic cathedrals and Wright's Prairie House development demonstrate, mediating sites of contemplation, where interpretation and representation work in tandem. Eisenman's emphasis on the plan – the figure–ground relationship – is the product of an established genealogy in Western architectural culture extending back, at the least, to Giambattista Nolli's 1748 engraving of the plan of Rome. However, what is distinctive is his treatment of the many drawn interpretations of the site as artificially excavated layers of archaeology, into which fictive and simulated layers are inserted or grafted to reinvigorate the characteristics of a place. Expanding on the two key Eisenman projects introduced in the previous chapter, we explored extensively how site connections were achieved. Instructive in this is Eisenman's skilful employment of *grafting* that began in site interpretation – the careful implantation of extraneous catalytic fragments, resulting in new relationships, inflecting both

158   Enis Aldallal | Site and Composition: Design strategies
       Husam AlWaer and | in architecture and urbanism
   Soumyen Bandyopadhyay |

the existing fragments and the graft. The grafting of the experiential through Laurie Olin's forecourt design, which makes references to American Prairie landscape and the Jeffersonian grid charting new territories, reconciles the abstract exploration of the horizontal with the equally abstract treatment of the vertical. The new 'betweenness' was extended further by the extension of the 15th Avenue, which now extends the campus into the city. At both Wexner and Aronoff, Eisenman successfully expanded on the true potential of the planimetric projective method by relying on a-textual fictive site formations resulting from manipulations and abstractions of site geometry. The mediatory properties of the 'betweenness' were illustrated further at Aronoff, where the architect sought to employ repetitions of the existing and proposed profiles in both plan and section to achieve a successful cohesion with surrounding landscape and structures.

The role of the edge condition formed the focus of discussions in Chapter 5, where we argued for the importance of reciprocity between interior and exterior spaces – between fragment and the whole – to achieve optimum integrity between site and context at differing scales. Returning to the ancient Greek idea of the *chora*, both as threshold between spaces and as receptacle for the virtual or imaginal qualities of space that underscore its 'materialisation' and physicality, we highlighted its contemporary relevance as a space of events. In achieving reciprocity the importance of considering flow or continuity is highlighted – whose trajectory we chart from modern to postmodern architecture – which was largely absent from early modern architecture, only to be overly rated, misunderstood and misused in later phases, as Leatherbarrow rightly suggests. At Alvaro Siza's Galician Centre for Contemporary Art, thresholds are established to mark transitions between the interior and the urban setting – yet these simultaneously distinguish and interrelate historical, urban and architectural events by anticipating and allowing movement *of* landscapes, as well as the flow of bodies *in* the landscape. Drawing

on a key example from late modern architecture – Le Corbusier's Mill Owners' Association Building in Ahmedabad – an interesting example of reciprocity in establishing a building's relationship with a virgin site is presented. Contrary to Wright's destruction of the 'box' to invite the outside in, here the partial dissolution of the box not only resulted in the outward flow of the interior contents but the flow through of the 'purified' Sabarmati river – *raison d'être* for the city of Ahmedabad, intended to connect also the cultural past with the future projected by post-independence aspirations.

Chapter 6 discussed the need for imaginative rethinking of materiality in achieving connections; to achieve a poetic wholeness we argued for both going beyond material manifestation with literal and immediate connectivity in mind, and also the dematerialisation of the architectural object and its setting. The material interpretation of both immediate context (a locale) and ultimate context (a region) was considered, as was the context prompted by earlier presences. Early modernist examples abound in their interest in achieving a dematerialised object, suspended in a void. This, however, was less important in the later phases of modernism, especially through the post-Second World War works of architects such as Aalto, Asplund, Kahn, Le Corbusier and so on. The key postmodern concern has been not only the seeking of material continuity with its immediate surroundings or even between technological advancement and tradition, but the need to engage with the demands and speeds of globalisation and the resultant demand for addressing diverse contexts as part of the idea of the region. Central to this is the interpretive intent as exemplified by the work of Herzog & de Meuron at CaixaForum. Earlier, in the late 1950s, extending the event space of the boundary, Charles Correa's work at the Gandhi Memorial Museum at Ahmedabad had blurred the boundary between inside and outside. This porosity, extending from imperviousness to expanding the boundary by turning it inside-out, is an important lesson for the postmodern era that expands the possibility of the membrane.

The implied possibility – or at least, the promise – to return to the 'thickness of things', presented through the remarkable and distinctive opportunities provided by orthogonal projections, highlights the analogical and scalar relationships that exist – and could exist – between the activity fragments of the city – sites – and the city as a whole. The instrumental and the existential, traditionally the domains of rationalists and phenomenologists, respectively, have long been treated as if they were mutually opposed political orientations. We argue for the instruments of both siting and composition – the methods of abstraction and codification in architecture – to return to their originally stated intentions of encapsulating deeper and more complex relationships between site and its wider context. The understanding of the reciprocatory nature of instruments and the phenomenon, co-mingled and coexistent, provide significant methodological and creative opportunities to students and architects in the early twenty-first century.

Architectural design research is at a critical crossroad. Much has been written recently regarding the state of architectural education and practice which, it has been argued, is losing its viability and relevance in the fast-changing world of globalisation and in the face of relentless production within the built environment at an unprecedented scale. The current political debate surrounding value for money in architectural projects has called into question the traditional approaches in architecture. The discussion surrounding the profession's social and cultural responsibilities and precisely what those might mean is yet another concern. While a number of these concerns may be well founded, the problem lies in the manner the discipline has chosen to respond to this situation of minor crisis. As in some previous instances, instead of addressing the issues and demands from within, the chosen approach generally has been to react by adopting extraneous instruments, approaches and aesthetic and technological devices. By imaginatively revisiting the instruments at the architect's disposal, it

is possible for architecture to mount a positive response to these issues. The discussions in this book revisit some of the limiting problems inherent in the architectural processes employed today and offer alternatives to enhance outputs. The intention here is to treat architecture and the city *not* as a collection of objects but as an overlapping network of relationships, cutting across temporal and cultural boundaries.

Illustration credits

162

Enis Aldallal
Husam AlWaer and
Soumyen Bandyopadhyay

Site and Composition: Design strategies
in architecture and urbanism

Photographs: *Enis Aldallal*: 1.2, 3.2–3.5, 3.8, 3.14, 3.16, 4.8–4.11, 4.13–4.15, 5.4a,b, 5.5, 5.7, 5.8, 6.4, 6.7; *Soumyen Bandyopadhyay*: 2.2, 2.3, 2.5, 2.6, 2.10–2.15, 2.18, 2.20, 3.7a, 5.12–5.20, 6.2, 6.8, 6.9a,b; *Richard Brook*: 6.5; *Clive Gracey*: 1.1; *Iain Jackson*: 2.1, 5.9, 5.11; *OTTO Archive*: 6.1; *Ana Souto*: 6.6.

Drawings and artwork: *Enis Aldallal*: 1.3, 1.4, 3.1, 3.2, 3.6, 3.7b, 3.9–3.13, 3.15, 3.17, 4.1–4.7, 4.12, 4.16, 4.17, 5.1–5.3, 5.6, 6.3, 6.12; *Soumyen Bandyopadhyay/Desiree Campolo* 5.10; *Desiree Campolo* 2.19, 5.21, 6.10, 6.11; *FLC/DACS* 2014: 2.7–2.9, 2.16, 2.17; *Iain Jackson*: 2.4.

Bibliography

166   Enis Aldallal | Site and Composition: Design strategies
Husam AlWaer and | in architecture and urbanism
Soumyen Bandyopadhyay |

Abercrombie, S. (1984) *Architecture as Art*, New York: Harper & Row.

AlWaer, H. (2014) 'Improving Contemporary Approaches to Master Planning Process', *Journal of Urban Design and Planning, Proceedings of the Institution of Civil Engineers* 167(1): 24–34.

AlWaer, H., Bickerton, R. & Kirk, R.D. (2014) 'Examining the Components Required for Assessing the Sustainability of Communities in the UK', *Journal of Architecture and Planning Research* 31(1): 1–26.

Amelar, S. (2006) 'Architecture and Art Building', *Architectural Record* 1/2006.

Andersen, K., 'Architecture & Design: A Crazy Building in Columbus – Peter Eisenman, Architecture's Bad Boy, Finally Hits his Stride', *Time,* 20 November 1989, www.kurtandersen.com/journalism/time/a-crazy-building-in-columbus, accessed 30 March 2015.

Architectural Association (2003) *Le Corbusier & the Architecture of Reinvention*, London: Architectural Association.

Architecture + Urbanism (A+U) (2008) 'CaixaForum, Madrid', *Architecture + Urbanism (A+U)* 5/2008.

Bandyopadhyay, S. (2011) *Manah: Omani Oasis, Arabian Legacy; Architecture and Social History of an Omani Oasis Settlement*, Liverpool: Liverpool University Press.

Bandyopadhyay, S. & Jackson, I. (2007) *The Collection, the Ruin and the Theatre: Architecture, Sculpture and Landscape in Nek Chand's Rock Garden, Chandigarh*, Liverpool: Liverpool University Press.

Barry, D. (1996) 'Connecting the Dots: The Dimensions of a Wire Frame', in Davidson, C. (ed.), *Eleven Authors in Search of a Building*, New York: Monacelli, pp. 48–59.

Beauregard, R. (2005) 'From Place to Site', in Burns, C. & Kahn, A. (eds), *Site Matters: Design Concepts, Histories and Strategies*, London: Routledge, pp. 39–58.

Bédard, J.-F. (ed.) (1994) *Cities of Artificial Excavation: The Work of Peter Eisenman, 1978–1988*, Montreal and New York: Canadian Centre for Architecture & Rizzoli International.

Bédard, J.-F. (1994) 'Introduction', in Bédard, J.-F. (ed.), *Cities of Artificial Excavation: The Work of Peter Eisenman, 1978–1988*, Montreal and New York: Canadian Centre for Architecture & Rizzoli International, pp. 9–18.

Benton, T. (2009) 'New Books on Le Corbusier', *Journal of Design History* 22(3): 271–284.

Bloomer, K. & Moore, C. (2006) 'Body, Memory, and Architecture', in Jencks, C. & Kropf, K. (eds), *Theories and Manifestoes of Contemporary Architecture* (second edition), London: Wiley Academy, pp. 71–74.

Blundell-Jones, P. (2006) *Gunnar Asplund*, London: Phaidon Press.

Bohm, D. (1980; 2012 reprint) *Wholeness and the Implicate Order*, London and New York: Routledge.

Bosworth, A. (1989) 'A Building Waiting to be a Building', *Columbus Monthly*, October.

Burns, C. & Kahn, A. (eds) (2005) *Site Matters: Design Concepts, Histories and Strategies*, New York and Abingdon: Routledge.

Carl, P. (2003) 'The Tower of Shadows', in *Architectural Association, Le Corbusier and the Architecture of Reinvention*, London: Architectural Association, pp. 98–117.

168   Enis Aldallal | Site and Composition: Design strategies
Husam AlWaer and | in architecture and urbanism
Soumyen Bandyopadhyay |

Ching, F. (1996) *Architecture: Form, Space, & Order*, New York: John Wiley.

Clark, R. & Pause, M. (2005) *Precedents in Architecture: Analytic Diagrams, Formative Ideas, and Partis*, Hoboken, NJ: John Wiley.

Cobb, H. (1996) 'A Note on the Criminology of Ornament: From Sullivan to Eisenman', in Davidson, C. (ed.), *Eleven Authors in Search of a Building*, New York: Monacelli Press, pp. 95–113.

Cohen, S. (1998) 'Physical Context/Cultural Context: Including it All', in Hays, M. (ed.), *Oppositions Reader: Selected Readings from a Journal for Ideas and Criticism in Architecture 1973–1984*, New York: Princeton Architectural Press, pp. 65–103.

Co-Intelligence Institute (2012) *Wholeness*. www.co-intelligence.org, accessed 21 December 2012.

Connah, R. (1989) *Writing Architecture: Fantômas Fragments Fictions – An Architectural Journey Through the Twentieth Century*, Cambridge, MA: MIT Press.

Correa, C. (1987) 'Transfer and Transformations', in Khan, H., *Charles Correa: Architect in India*, Singapore and London: Mimar/Butterworth Architecture, pp. 165–175.

Davidson, C. (ed.) (1996) *Eleven Authors in Search of a Building*, New York: Monacelli Press.

Davidson, C. (2006) *Tracing Eisenman*, New York: Thames & Hudson.

Dodds, G. (2002) 'Desiring Landscapes/Landscapes of Desire: Scopic and Somatic in the Brion Sanctuary', in Dodds, G. & Tavernor, R. (eds), *Body and Building: Essays on the Changing Relation of Body and Architecture*, Cambridge, MA: MIT Press, pp. 238–257.

Dovey, K. (1999) *Framing Places: Mediating Power in Built Form*, New York: Routledge.

Dripps, R. (2005) 'Groundwork', in Burns, C. & Kahn, A. (eds), *Site Matters: Design Concepts, Histories and Strategies*, New York and Abingdon: Routledge, pp. 59–92.

Eisenman, P. (1998) 'Aspects of Modernism: Maison Dom-ino and the Self-Referential Sign', in Hays, M. (ed.), *Oppositions Reader: Selected Readings from a Journal for Ideas and Criticism in Architecture 1973–1984*, New York: Princeton Architectural Press, pp. 188–199.

Eisenman, P. (1989) 'Cincinnati University', *El Croquis* 41: 100–105.

Eisenman, P. (1989) 'Wexner Centre', *El Croquis* 41: 30–51.

Eisenman, P. & Bédard, J.-F. (1994) 'Cannaregio: Submission to the International Seminar of Design for Cannaregio West, Venice, 1978', in Bédard, J.-F. (ed.), *Cities of Artificial Excavation: The Work of Peter Eisenman, 1978–1988*, Montreal and New York: Canadian Centre for Architecture & Rizzoli International, pp. 46–71.

Eisenman, P. with Balfour, A., Bédard, J.-F., Bois, Y.-A., Cohen, J.-F., Hays, M., & Olsberg, N., (1998) 'Conversation with Peter Eisenman', in Bédard, J.-F. (ed.), *Cities of Artificial Excavation: The Work of Peter Eisenman, 1978–1988*, Montreal and New York: Canadian Centre for Architecture & Rizzoli International, pp. 118–129.

El Croquis/Hadid, Z. (2004) *Zaha Hadid (1983–2004): El Croquis 53/73 (I)/103*, Madrid: El Croquis.

Ellin, N. (2006) *Integral Urbanism*, London and New York: Taylor & Francis.

Ellis, W. (1998) 'Type and Context in Urbanism: Colin Rowe's Contextualism', in Hays, M. (ed.), *Oppositions Reader: Selected Readings from a Journal for Ideas and Criticism in Architecture 1973–1984*, New York: Princeton Architectural Press, pp. 227–251.

Evans, R. (1995) *The Projective Cast: Architecture and its Three Geometries*, Cambridge, MA: MIT Press.

Evenson, N. (1989) *The Indian Metropolis: A View Toward the West*, New Haven, CT: Yale University Press.

Ferguson, J. (Burgess, J. & Spiers, R., eds) (1876; second Indian edition, 1972) *History of Indian and Eastern Architecture 1*, Delhi: Munshiram Monoharlal.

Flam, J. (ed.) (1996) *Robert Smithson: The Collected Writings*, Berkeley, CA: University of California Press.

Forster. K. (1996) 'Rising from the Land, Sinking into the Ground', in Davidson, C. (ed.), *Eleven Authors in Search of a Building*, New York: Monacelli Press, pp. 114–133.

Forty, A. (2000) *Words and Buildings: A Vocabulary of Modern Architecture*, London: Thames & Hudson.

Frampton, K. (2006) 'Towards a Critical Regionalism: Six Points for an Architecture of Resistance', in Jencks, C. & Kropf, K. (eds), *Theories and Manifestoes of Contemporary Architecture* (second edition), London: Wiley Academy, pp. 97–100.

Frampton, K. (2000) 'Architecture as Critical Transformation: The Work of Álvaro Siza', in Frampton, K. & Siza, A., *Alvaro Siza: Complete Works*, London: Phaidon, pp. 11–65.

Frampton, K. (1983) 'Prospects for a Critical *Regionalism*', *Perspecta* 20: 147–162.

Frampton, K. (1975) 'Le Corbusier and the Dialectical Imagination', *Global Architecture* 37: 2–7.

Frampton, K. & Siza, A. (2000) *Alvaro Siza: Complete Works*, London: Phaidon.

Franck, K. & Lepori, B. (2007) *Architecture from the Inside Out: From the Body, the Senses, the Site, and the Community*, London: Wiley Academy.

Frascari, M. (2002) 'A Tradition of Architectural Figures: A Search for Vita Beata', in Dodds, G. & Tavernor, R. (eds), *Body and Building: Essays on the Changing Relation of Body and Architecture*, Cambridge, MA: MIT Press, pp. 258–267.

Frascari, M., Hale, J. & Starkey, B. (eds) (2007) *From Models to Drawings: Imagination and Representation in Architecture*, London: Routledge.

Fredwest, J. http://daapspace4.daap.uc.edu/~larsongr/Larsonline/Eisenman_files/Eisen-DAAP.pdf, accessed 20 November 2007.

Grassi, G. (1998) 'Avant-Garde and Continuity', in Hays, M. (ed.), *Oppositions Reader: Selected Readings from a Journal for Ideas and Criticism in Architecture 1973–1984*, New York: Princeton Architectural Press, pp. 390–399.

Graves, M. (2006) 'A Case for Figurative Architecture', in Jencks, C. & Kropf, K. (eds), *Theories and Manifestoes of Contemporary Architecture* (second edition), London: Wiley Academy, p. 93.

Green, J. (1989) 'Algorithms for Discovery', in Moneo, R. & Vidler, A. (eds), *Wexner Centre for the Visual Arts*, New York: Rizzoli, pp. 28–31.

Grosz, E. (2001) *Architecture from the Outside*, Cambridge, MA: MIT Press.

170   Enis Aldallal | Site and Composition: Design strategies
Husam AlWaer and | in architecture and urbanism
Soumyen Bandyopadhyay |

Hadid, Z. (2006) 'The Eighty-Nine Degrees', in Jencks, C. & Kropf, K. (eds), *Theories and Manifestoes of Contemporary Architecture* (second edition), London: Wiley Academy, p. 280. Extract from: Hadid, Z. (1983) Planetary Architecture Two, London: Architectural Association, unpaginated.

Hadid, Z. (2006) 'Explosions; Compressions; Swarms, Aggressions, Pixelations; Carved Spaces, Excavations', in Jencks, C. & Kropf, K. (eds), *Theories and Manifestoes of Contemporary Architecture*, London: Wiley Academy, pp. 364–365. Extract from: Hadid, Z. (2004) 'Explosions…' in Fontana-Giusti, G. & Schumacher, P. (eds), *Zaha Hadid: The Complete Works: Projects Documentations* (1/4). London: Thames & Hudson.

Hartoonian, G. (2006) *The Crisis of the Object: The Architecture of Theatricality*, New York: Routledge.

Hays, M. (ed.) (1998) *Oppositions Reader: Selected Readings from a Journal for Ideas and Criticism in Architecture 1973– 1984*, New York: Princeton Architectural Press.

Hearn, M. (2003) *Ideas that Shaped Buildings*, Cambridge, MA: MIT Press.

Herbert, D. (1992) 'Graphic Process in Architectural Style Study Drawings', *Journal of Architectural Education* 46(1): 28–39.

Hill, J. (2005) 'Building the Drawing', *Architectural Design* (Special issue: *Design Through Making*) 75(4): 13–21.

Hodder, I. (1986) *Reading the Past: Current Approaches to Interpretation in Archaeology*, Cambridge: Cambridge University Press.

Hoffmann, D. (1984) *Frank Lloyd Wright's Robie House: The Illustrated Story of an Architectural Masterpiece*, New York: Dover Publications.

Hogue, M. (2004) 'The Site as Project: Lessons from Land Art and Conceptual Art', *Journal of Architectural Education* 57(3): 54–61.

Holl, S. (2007) 'Questions of Perception: Phenomenology of Architecture', in Holl, S., Pallasmaa, J. & Pérez Gómez, A., *A+U: Questions of Perception: Phenomenology of Architecture*, San Francisco: William Stout Publishers, pp. 44–46.

Holl, S., Pallasmaa, J. & Gómez, A. (1994, 2007 reprint) *Questions of Perception: Phenomenology of Architecture*, Tokyo: A+U Publishing; San Francisco: William Stout Publishers.

Isenstadt, S. (2005) 'Contested Context', in Burns, C. & Kahn, A. (eds), *Site Matters: Design Concepts, Histories and Strategies*, London: Routledge, pp. 157–184.

Jameson, F. (1994) 'Modernity Versus Postmodernity in Peter Eisenman', in Bédard, J.-F. (ed.), *Cities of Artificial Excavation: The Work of Peter Eisenman, 1978–1988*, Montreal and New York: Canadian Centre for Architecture & Rizzoli International, pp. 27–37.

Jeanneret, M. (2001) *Perpetual Motion: Transforming Shapes in the Renaissance from da Vinci to Montaigne*, Baltimore, MD: Johns Hopkins University Press.

Jencks, C. (1987) *Le Corbusier and the Tragic View of Architecture*, Harmondsworth: Penguin.

Jencks, C. & Kropf, K. (eds) (2006) *Theories and Manifestoes of Contemporary Architecture* (second edition), London: Wiley Academy.

Jones, K. (1990) 'The Wexner Fragments for the Visual Arts', *Journal of Architectural Education* 43(3): 34–38.

Kalia, R. (1999) *Chandigarh: The Making of an Indian City*, New Delhi: Oxford University Press.

Khan, H. (ed.) (1987) *Charles Correa: Architect in India*, London: Mimar/Butterworth Architecture.

Kolbowski, S. (1996) 'Fringe Benefits', in Davidson, C. (ed.), *Eleven Authors in Search of a Building*, New York: Monacelli, pp. 134–151.

Kries, M. (2007) 'S, M, L, XL: Metamorphoses of the Orient in the Work of Le Corbusier', in von Vegesack, A., von Moos, S., Rüegg, A. & Kries, M. (eds), *Le Corbusier: The Art of Architecture*, Weil am Rhein: Vitra, pp. 163–208.

Leatherbarrow, D. (2009) *Architecture Oriented Otherwise*, New York: Princeton Architectural Press.

Leatherbarrow, D. (2004) *Topographical Stories: Studies in Landscape and Architecture*, Pennsylvania: University of Pennsylvania Press.

Leatherbarrow, D. (2004) 'Topographical Premises', *Journal of Architectural Education*, 57(3): 70–73.

Leatherbarrow, D. (2002) *Uncommon Ground: Architecture, Technology, and Topography*, Cambridge, MA: MIT Press.

Leatherbarrow, D. (1993) *The Roots of Architectural Invention: Site, Enclosure, Materials*, Cambridge: Cambridge University Press.

Le Corbusier (Hylton, K., trans.) (2003) '*Poème de l'Angle Droit*', in Architectural Association, *Le Corbusier and the Architecture of Reinvention*, London: Architectural Association, pp. 58–97

Le Corbusier (Žaknić, I., trans.) (1987) *Journey to the East*, Cambridge, MA: MIT Press.

Le Corbusier (1982) *Le Corbusier Sketchbooks*, London and Paris: Thames & Hudson/Fondation Le Corbusier.

Libeskind, D. (2006) 'Unoriginal Signs', in Jencks, C. & Kropf, K. (eds), *Theories and Manifestoes of Contemporary Architecture* (second edition), London: Wiley Academy, p. 281. Extract from: Libeskind, D. 1983. *Chamber Works*. London: Architectural Association.

Lynch, K. (1984) *Site Planning*, Cambridge, MA: MIT Press.

Lynn, G. (2006) 'The City of Culture of Galicia', in Davidson, C. (ed.), *Tracing Eisenman*, London: Thames & Hudson, pp. 308–318.

Maymind, A. (2014) 'Still Ugly After All These Years: A Close Reading of Peter Eisenman's Wexner Center'. http://archinect.com/features/article/49090085/still-ugly-after-all-these-years-a-close-reading-of-peter-eisenman-s-wexner-center, accessed 26 May 2014.

Mayne, T. (2006) 'Connected Isolation', in Jencks, C. & Kropf, K. (eds), *Theories and Manifestoes of Contemporary Architecture* (second edition), London: Wiley Academy, pp. 301–303. Extract from: Mayne, T. & Morphosis (1993) Morphosis: Connected Isolation. Architectural Monographs 23. London: Academy Editions.

Mayr, B. (2005) 'Architect Likes What He Sees at Wexner', *The Columbus Dispatch*, 1 November, E3.

Meirav, A. (2003) *Wholes, Sums and Unities*, London: Springer.

Melhuish, C. (2001) 'Art and Architecture: The Dynamics of Collaboration', in Trasi, N. (ed.), *Interdisciplinary Architecture*, London: Wiley Academy, pp. 22–27.

Meyer, E. (2005) 'Site Citations', in Burns, C. & Kahn, A. (eds) *Site Matters: Design Concepts, Histories and Strategies*, London: Routledge, pp. 93–130.

Moneo, R. (2004) *Theoretical Anxiety and Design Strategies in the Work of Eight Contemporary Architects*, Cambridge, MA: MIT Press.

Moneo, R. (1989) 'Unexpected Coincidences', in Moneo, R. & Vidler, A. (eds), *Wexner Centre for the Visual Arts, the Ohio State University*, New York: Rizzoli, pp. 40–45. Also published as, Moneo, R. (1989) 'Unexpected Coincidences (Inesperadas Coincidencias)', *El Croquis* 41: 52–61.

Moneo, R. & Vidler, A. (eds) (1989) *Wexner Centre for the Visual Arts, the Ohio State University*, New York: Rizzoli.

Morson, G. & Emerson, C. (1990) *Mikhail Bakhtin: Creation of a Prosaics*, Stanford, CA: Stanford University Press.

Moughtin, C., Oc, T. & Tiesdell, S. (2001) 'Colour in the City', in Trasi, N. (ed.), *Interdisciplinary Architecture*, London: Wiley Academy, pp. 68–71.

Muschamp, H. (2000) Art/Architecture; How Modern Design Remains Faithful to its Context', *New York Times*, 6 August 2000. http://query.nytimes.com/gst/fullpage.html?res=9B0DE4DD113DF935A3575BC0A9669C8B63&sec=&spon=&pagewanted=all, accessed 30 March 2015.

Nas, P. (ed.) (1993) *Urban Symbolism 8*, New York and Leiden: Brill.

Nehru, J. (1946, 1982 reprint) *The Discovery of India*, Calcutta: Signet Press.

Norberg-Schulz, C. (Nasso, C. & Parini, S., eds; Shugaar, A., trans.) (2000) *Architecture: Presence, Language and Place*, Milan: Skira.

Norberg-Schulz, C. (1965) *Intentions in Architecture*, Cambridge, MA: MIT Press.

Onians, J. (2002) 'Greek Temple and Greek Brain', in Dodds, G. & Tavernor, R. (eds), *Body and Building: Essays on the Changing Relation of Body and Architecture*, Cambridge, MA: MIT Press, pp. 44–63.

Pallasmaa, J. (2007) 'An Architecture of the Seven Senses', in Holl, S., Pallasmaa, J. & Pérez Gómez, A., *A+U: Questions of Perception: Phenomenology of Architecture*, San Francisco, CA: William Stout Publishers, pp. 27–39.

Perera, N. (2004) 'Contesting Visions: Hybridity, Liminality and Authorship of the Chandigarh Plan', *Planning Perspectives* 19(2): 175–199.

Pérez Gómez, A. (2007) 'The Space of Architecture: Meaning as Presence and Representation', in Holl, S., Pallasmaa, J. & Pérez Gómez, A., *A+U: Questions of Perception: Phenomenology of Architecture*, San Francisco, CA: William Stout Publishers, pp. 7–26.

Pritzker Architecture Prize, www.pritzkerprize.com/2004/pdf/LFOne.pdf, accessed 6 February 2008.

Rasmussen, E. (1959) *Experiencing Architecture*, London: Chapman and Hall.

Redfield, W. (2005) 'The Suppressed Site: Revealing the Influence of Site on Two Purist Works', in Burns, C. & Kahn, A. (eds), *Site Matters: Design Concepts, Histories and Strategies*, London: Routledge, pp. 185–222.

Robbins, E. (1994) *Why Architects Draw*, Cambridge, MA: MIT Press.

Rossi, A. (1982; 1984 paperback) *The Architecture of the City*, Cambridge, MA: MIT Press.

Roth, L. (2006) *Understanding Architecture: Its Elements, History, and Meaning*, Boulder, CO: Westview Press.

RoTo Architecture, 'Architecture and Art Building, Prairie View, A&M University', www.rotoark.com/projects/education-cultural-civic/prairie-view-university; accessed 11 April 2015.

Rykwert, J. (2006) 'Ornament is no Crime', in Rykwert, J., *The Necessity of Artifice*, London: Academy Editions, pp. 92–101.

Rykwert, J. (1982) *The Necessity of Artifice*, London: Academy Editions.

Rykwert, J. (1982) 'The Necessity of Artifice', in Rykwert, J., *The Necessity of Artifice*, London: Academy Editions, pp. 58–59.

Salingaros, N.A. (2000) 'Complexity and Urban Coherence', *Journal of Urban Design* 5(3): 291–316.

Sarin, M. (1982) *Urban Planning in the Third World: The Chandigarh Experience*, London: Mansell.

Sassi, P. (2012) *Strategies for Sustainable Architecture*, London: Taylor & Francis.

Scafer, R. (2008) 'Landscape', in Wingardh, G. & Wærn, R. (eds), *Crucial Words: Conditions for Contemporary Architecture*, Berlin: Birkhauser, pp. 110–113.

Schildt, G. (1998) *Alvar Aalto in His Own Words*, New York: Rizzoli.

Schneider, P. (2007) 'Disegno: On Drawing Out the Architexts', *Journal of Architectural Education* 61(1): 19–22.

Schumacher, T. (2005) 'Horizontality: The Modernist Line', *Journal of Architectural Education* 59(1): 17–26.

Sharr, A. (2007) *Thinkers for Architects: Heidegger for Architects*, New York: Routledge.

Sklair, L., 'Iconic Architecture and Capitalist Globalisation', in Herrle, P. & Wegerhoff, E. (eds), *Architecture and Identity*, Berlin: LIT Verlag, 2008, pp. 210–219.

Smith, P. (1987) *Architecture and the Principle of Harmony*, London: RIBA Publications.

Smith, P. (1977) *The Syntax of Cities*, London: Hutchinson.

Smith, P. (1974) *The Dynamics of Urbanism*, London: Hutchinson.

Sorkin, M. (1989) 'Solid Geometry', *House & Garden* 10/1989: 62–66.

Spens, M. (2007) 'Site/Non-Site: Extending the Parameters in Contemporary Landscape', *Architectural Design* 77(2): 6–11.

Stearns, R. (1989) 'Building as Catalyst', in Moneo, R. & Vidler, A. (eds), *Wexner Centre for the Visual Arts, the Ohio State University*, New York: Rizzoli, pp. 24–27.

Talen, E. (2005) 'Evaluating Good Urban Form in an Inner-city Neighborhood: An Empirical Application', *Journal of Architectural and Planning Research* 22(3): 204–228.

Tan, T. & Kudaisya, G. (2000) *The Aftermath of Partition of South Asia*, London: Routledge.

Tavernor, R. (1998) *On Alberti and the Art of Building*, New Haven, CT: Yale University Press.

Temple, N. (2007) *Disclosing Horizons: Architecture, Perspective and Redemptive Space*, London and New York: Routledge.

Temple, N. & Bandyopadhyay, S. (2007) 'Contemplating the Unfinished: Architectural Drawing and the Fabricated Ruin', in Marco, F., Jonathan, H. and Bradley, S. (eds), *From Models*

174   Enis Aldallal | Site and Composition: Design strategies
Husam AlWaer and | in architecture and urbanism
Soumyen Bandyopadhyay |

to Drawings: Imagination and Representation in Architecture, London: Routledge, pp. 109–119.

Trancik, R. (1986) Finding Lost Space, New York: Van Nostrand Reinhold.

Tronzo, W. (ed.) (2009) The Fragment: An Incomplete History, Los Angeles: Getty Publications.

Tschumi, B. (2004) Event-Cities 3, Cambridge, MA: MIT Press.

Tschumi, B. (1996; 2004 reprint) Architecture and Disjunction, Cambridge, MA: MIT Press.

Venturi, R. (1966; 1977 reprint) Complexity and Contradiction in Architecture, New York: Museum of Modern Art.

Vesely, D. (2004) Architecture in the Age of Divided Representation: The Question of Creativity in the Shadow of Production, Cambridge, MA: MIT Press.

Vidler, A. (2001) Warped Space: Art, Architecture, and Anxiety in Modern Culture, Cambridge, MA: MIT Press.

Vidler, A. (1989) 'Counter-Monuments in Practice: The Wexner Centre for the Visual Arts', in Wexner Centre for the Visual Arts, the Ohio State University, New York: Rizzoli, pp. 32–38.

Weston, R. (2003) Materials, Form and Architecture, London: Laurence King.

Wheeler, B.M. (2006) Mecca and Eden: Ritual, Relics, and Territory in Islam, Chicago, IL: University of Chicago Press.

Whiting, S. (1996) 'Building Inside Out: Perspectives on the Conspicuously Inconspicuous', in Davidson, C. (ed.), Eleven Authors in Search of a Building, New York: Monacelli, pp. 98–107.

Yoshida, N. & Zumthor, P. (1998) A+U: Peter Zumthor, February 1998 extra edition, Tokyo: A+U Publishing.

Yoshizaka, T. (1974) 'Chandigarh: A Few Thoughts on How Le Corbusier Tackled His Work', in Le Corbusier: Chandigarh, The New Capital of Punjab, India 1951–, Tokyo: A.D.A. Edita, pp. 2–7.

Zevi, B. (1957) Architecture as Space, New York: Horizon Press.

Index

176   Enis Aldallal | Site and Composition: Design strategies
Husam AlWaer and | in architecture and urbanism
Soumyen Bandyopadhyay

178   Enis Aldallal | Site and Composition: Design strategies
Husam AlWaer and | in architecture and urbanism
Soumyen Bandyopadhyay

180   Enis Aldallal | Site and Composition: Design strategies
Husam AlWaer and | in architecture and urbanism
Soumyen Bandyopadhyay

182   Enis Aldallal | Site and Composition: Design strategies
Husam AlWaer and | in architecture and urbanism
Soumyen Bandyopadhyay